Table of Contents:

1.1. Introduction of Slow Cooker   4
1.2. Design and Operation
1.3. Maintenance and Care
1.4. Advantages   9
1.5. Disadvantages   10
1.6. Cooking Tips   11

2.1. Recipes

1. Slow Cooked Pumpkin Pie Pudding   14
2. Fudgy Brownie with strawberry   16
3. Crust less Lemon Cheesecake   19
4. Chocolate bread pudding   22
5. Spicy Fruit Compote   24
6. Rice Pudding   26
7. Chocolaty Walnut bread pudding   28
8. Strawberry Cheesecake   30
9. Peach Cobbler   32
10. Slow cooked Chocolate Fondue   34
11. White Chocolate Bread Pudding   36
12. Blackberry Cobbler with sweet cornbread   38
13. Slow Cooker Apple Butter   40
14. Peanut Chocolate candy   42
15. Pineapple Upside Down Cake   44
16. Slow cooker Carrot Cake   46
17. Lemon – Poppy seed Cake   48
18. Sour Cream Cheesecake   50
19. Apple Granola   53
20. Bananas Foster   55

21. Double Apple Cake   57
22. Spicy Poached Pear   59
23. Mixed Berry Compote (over Angel food Cake)   61
24. Cinnamon – Raisin Bread Pudding   63
25. Chocolate Brownie Sundaes   65
26. Pecan Pie   67
27. Rich Hot Fudge Cake   69
28. Pina Colada Lava Cake   71
29. Marshmallow Brownie   73
30. Almond and Plum Cake   75
31. Chocolate Scones   78
32. Crumbled Hazelnut Cheesecake   80
33. Pecan Buns   83
34. Chocolate Cherry Cake   86
35. Cherry Cobbler   88
36. Pavlova with Fruit   90
37. Coconut Cake   92
38. Crock pot Apple Pie   94
39. Crunchy Chocolaty Nutella Cheesecake   96
40. Pumpkin Cheesecake   99
41. Sweet Pecan Candy   102
42. Dulce De Leche   104

Other Best-Sellers from this Author:

1.1. Introduction of Slow Cooker:

Slow cooker or Crock-pot is just another electric cooking appliance that can cook healthy and delicious food. However, the most interesting feature of this cooking appliance is that it offers almost fully unattended cooking. Most importantly, with a slow cooker handy, you can expect a freshly cooked, warm meal waiting for you in the kitchen when you come back from office or when you wake up in the morning. It surely sounds amazing, doesn't it?

Slow cooker has a few truly amazing features that can make this possible for you. It has a timer that can be set in advance according to the cooking process needed for a dish. Few models of slow cooker even come with software installed in it with which you can program the sequences of cooking process and be worry free. Slow cooking needs a very little preparation time from your side. For example: You can arrange the ingredients in the cooker pot and program the settings and turn it on just before you are going to sleep or leaving for office. All the rest will be taken care by the slow cooker. It will keep cooking for hours, without allowing the food to burn and it's safe to use in any household. It is good for making soups, stews, boiled meals and also for baking, frying etc.

In short, you can cook almost everything in it. It cooks with low heat setting, provides uniform heating and keeps the food warm for hours. This concept of using slow cooker for making meals is particularly popular in US, Canada, New Zealand and Australia, however, its popularity and the flavor of its goodness is spreading throughout the world slowly and it is predicted that it is going to be the most admired and popular cooking style of the current century.

1.2. Design and Operation:

It is an oval or round lidded pot made with porcelain or glazed ceramic. A metal wire surrounds it through which heat can be generated with electrical charges. The lid is generally made of glass and placed on the grooved edge of the pot. Vapor concentrates in the groove and creates a mild atmospheric pressure outside of the pot, which in turn, balances the water vapor pressure created inside the pot. This eliminates the chance of any sudden release of vapor. This pressure balance mechanism makes this cooker different and safer from the regular pressure cooker.

The main cooking area, the pot or the ceramic vessel is designed in such way that it can maintain steady heat. The capacity of the pot may vary from 500 ml (16 oz) to 7 liters (7.4 US quarts). There is a liquid level indicator which is to protect the cooker from uncontrolled heating. The recommended liquid level should be maintained always for safety.

Generally, a slow cooker has two or more temperature settings levels like, 'low', 'warm', 'medium', 'high', 'keep warm' etc. Few slow cookers come with continuous power variation mechanism. Other types of slow cookers don't have any temperature control settings and provide constant heat for several hours.

While cooking raw ingredients and a liquid of your choice (water, stock or wine etc) are arranged in the pot. For some recipes already warm liquid may be added. Then the lid is put on it and cooker is switched on.

Some cookers keep on cooking at same temperature and some may automatically switch from cooking mode to warming mode (71–74 °C / 160–165 °F). There is a probe inserted to measure the temperature which determines the switching point between different modes.

The heat of material inside the pot is maintained generally at temperature from 79–93 °C (175–200 °F) during cooking.
It can be adjusted according to the need of the recipe. Vapor produced from the heat inside the pot accumulates near the lid and turns into liquid and comes back. Some vitamins (water soluble) are filtered into the liquid. The lid helps prevent the vapor from escaping from the content while cooking and also while cooling. The liquid passes the heat from vessel wall to the raw ingredients and also spreads the flavor.

Some slow cookers need to be manually switched on and off, before and after cooking whereas others have automatic function for these activities.

The most efficient and latest slow cookers even have computerized control operations (e.g. you can program and set cooking for two hours on high, two hours on medium, two hours on low and then keep warm for another two hours and switch it off and also can set a timer to delay the start of cooking). That's what is called proper effortless cooking.

As the food cooked in the crock-pot remains warm in it for long, the effort in re-heating your prepared meal can be eliminated. You can also carry your crock-pot with you along with the prepared meal without the fear of the food spilling out of the pot as the lid of the cooker can be sealed fully.

As the slow cooker operates completely different, regular recipes should be modified a bit to cook in it. Liquid quantity should be manipulated according to the evaporation rate in slow cooker and also one should see that the container has enough liquid for the quantity of food. The dishes cooked in a slow cooker turn out to be really scrumptious.

1.3. Maintenance and care:

As with any other trusty appliance, a slow cooker needs special care and maintenance.

- → It can only be disassembled for cleaning by the user. For any repair work or anything else, disassembling should be done by experts. For servicing, always call professional appliance service men.
- → Abrupt temperature changes should be avoided. When the glass lid or the stoneware is hot, do not suddenly put them in cold water or keep them on any wet platform.
- → The container shouldn't be used for storing the food in refrigerator. If for some reason you have done that, then please remember not to re-heat it immediately after taking it out from refrigerator. Abrupt temperature changes may cause your stoneware to crack.
- → If you notice any crack on the stoneware or on the lid, then do not use it. It is no longer safe.
- → Keep it clean always.

Cleaning:

- → The base unit of the cooker and the plug should never be immersed in water. Keep them aside while cleaning.
- → Never forget to unplug the cooker from any electrical source and let it cool fully before starting the cleaning process.
- → You can clean the glass lid and the stoneware in the dishwasher. Keep the stoneware away from other utensils in the dishwasher to make sure it does not get damaged.
- → To remove leftover food or food stains from stoneware, fill it up with lukewarm soap water and leave it soak for 10-15 minutes. Take some baking soda on a plastic scouring pad

(Do not use steelwool or you will scratch your stoneware) and apply it on the surface of the cooker while cleaning.
→ Apply distilled white vinegar to wipe out any water stain or mineral accumulation inside the stoneware. If the stain is deep, apply a little vinegar, let it soak for few minutes, rinse it and then let it dry.
→ Take a damp, soft cloth to wipe both inside and outside of the base unit. Never use rough clothes or cleaners as the surface may get damaged.

1.4. Advantages:

There is no doubt that the slow cooker has a lot of advantages compared to other cooking appliances. Here are some benefits:

a) Slow cooking can soften the lean muscles and connective tissues of meat that is very useful part of making healthy and tasty stews. On other cooking processes, these muscles and tissues are removed because they toughen the meat while cooking. A slow cooker helps maintain the food's integrity in a dish to its maximum possible level.
b) With adequate liquids, there is little to no chance for your meal to get burnt while cooking for so long because of the low temperature setting and uniform heating process of a slow cooker.
c) The timer of the slow cooker is very useful. You can even set the timer to start the cooking process at your convenience. Suppose you are leaving for office at 7 am, but you want the slow cooker to start cooking at 9 am. You can actually set the timer accordingly and cook your dish according to your preferred time, so that when you come back from office you get a nice, hot meal ready for you.
d) The slow cooker is amazing in keeping the food warm in it for long hours even after the cooking process is finished.
e) Crock-pot makes one pot meal, which spares us from cleaning many pots and pans after cooking. Moreover, its design with detachable parts makes the cleaning and maintenance process simpler.
f) To a certain degree, the slow cooker is safer than stove tops and ovens because its temperature remains much lower during the whole process of cooking.

1.5. Disadvantages:

Does a slow cooker really have any disadvantages? We wonder, really. It sounds crazy, but it's true that it has a very few drawbacks like any other appliances.

a) Many vegetables lose their vitamins and trace nutrients during the cooking process. However, as slow cooker has relatively low temperature settings, it partially prevents good enzymes from getting denatured compared to other high temperature cooking processes. Using blanched or pre-cooked vegetables may help to keep the vitamins and nutrients intact in vegetables.
b) Foods cooked in slow cooker should not be allowed to cool below 70 °C (158 °F) as at this temperature harmful bacteria can grow inside the cooker and spoil the food. Few of these harmful bacteria may even produce spores and toxins which don't go away even after re-heating.
c) If you have ingredients to be added at the last stage of cooking, then again you have to wait for long hours to allow that ingredient to cook thoroughly as slow cooker takes long time to cook each and every ingredient. However, it is worth waiting, because the outcome will be so scrumptious.

1.6. General Cooking Tips:

Here are a few handful slow cooker cooking tips that will help you cook more easily to get more satisfying, rich and aromatic meals at all times. Follow these tips and get expertise in slow cooking.

a) **Keep crock-pot lid closed:** If you are at home and making the day meal in slow cooker, then you may tend to peek at the food and stir it, while cooking process is on. However, it would be better if you can control yourself from peeking frequently and from stirring the food in between. Because every time you open the lid, you slow down the cooking process by at least 10 – 15 minutes. So, the more you stir it, it would take more time to cook and will test your patience. You may also get delayed for serving the meal for your family or guests. Slow cooker needs very little or no attention or supervision during cooking. So, it's you who have to minimize the number of stirring, keep the lid closed and your meal will be ready on time.

b) **Do not allow abrupt shift of temperature of the crock:** Never put a hot ceramic insert into the cold counter, as it may lead to cracks. If you have to do that in any case, then first put dish towel in the counter before placing the hot ceramic insert.

c) **Opt for browning:** Instead of just arranging the ingredients in the crock pot, turning the cooker on and getting a dish ready, opt for browning prior to cooking. This improves taste, flavor and texture. This trick can be perfectly applied for meats (ground or shredded) and sauces. The meat gets additional flavor and texture; and sauces get more thickness when browned in advance before putting them in the slow cooker pot.

d) **Avoid using frozen ingredients**: Except pre-packed, frozen, ready-made slow cooker meals, avoid using any other frozen items while cooking in slow cooker. The items must be thawed properly before you put them in crock-pot. Otherwise there is a chance for the bacteria to get flourished.
e) **Do not overload the cooker:** Make sure you fill the cooker pot by half or max by two-third of its size with ingredients and liquid. If you fill the pot beyond this, it will get overloaded and you may not get desired or satisfying result. For roasting a big chicken or something like that, use a bigger cooker to maintain the ratio.
f) **Cut off fat and skin:** Trimming the fat parts and also the skin from meat will yield less oily and greasy cooking liquid.
g) **Layer evenly:** Use uniformly cut vegetables to allow uniform cooking. If you are using root vegetables like carrots, potatoes etc, then put them as bottom layer and arrange the meat on top of that layer to get best results.
h) **Beware while using dairy items**: Dairy products tend to break down during slow cooking. So, add them in last 15 minutes of cooking and keep stirring meanwhile.
i) **Maintain heat level:** Few recipes cook well in high heat settings and few other tastes better when cooked on low heat settings. So, choose and maintain the heat level accordingly. Generally low heat setting operates around 170°F and high heat setting operates around 280°F.
j) **Finishing Touch:** For any slow cooked dishes, you can sprinkle some fresh herbs or just squeeze juice of a lemon. This will enhance the richness and flavor of the food. Other choices of garnishing may be like grated parmesan cheese, hot sauce, olive oil, sautéed garlic, citrus zest etc.

A few Dessert specific tips:

a) While baking a cake in a slow cooker, it is good idea to put tea towels or paper towels under the cooker lid to capture moisture and water dripping from the top. Dripping water on the cake may make it soggy.
b) Using Non-stick cooking spray is a must for baking in the slow cooker.
c) Using baking paper to line the crock pot makes it easy to remove cake or other baked products from the cooker.
d) In order to know whether baking is complete or not you can carry out the toothpick test. Just before cooking cycle is finished, insert a toothpick at the center of the pot and see if it comes out clean. If it feels sticky, then you may have to continue cooking and if it comes out clean it indicates that the center of the cake is set well and the cooking is done.
e) If you are making slow cooker cheesecake for dessert then it is good idea to refrigerate it or allow it to chill before serving. Chilling improves the texture of the cheesecake.

2.1. Recipes

If you have got an impression so far, that slow cooker can only offer quick and easy meal, and nothing beyond that, think twice. How about baking a cake or making berry stuffed apple for dessert? Is it sounding tempting already? If yes, then indulge yourself in the next section, because a pool of luscious dessert recipes is here to blow your mind away.

1. Slow Cooked Pumpkin Pie Pudding

Don't let your fabulous evening dinner go flop only because you forgot to cook the dessert. A nice dessert can complete your meal nicely. There is a 'feel good' factor in this. And when you have a slow cooker handy, you don't need to put any effort in making your dessert at all. Just plan it and leave it to slow cooker. This particular dessert is meant for the pumpkin lovers. It is sweetish and creamy, promises to satisfy your taste buds after a meal. Slow cooker recipes are always easy and so is this one. Look at the recipe and you will love it.

Preparation Time: 10 minutes

Cooking Time: 6 hours

Recommended Slow Cooker size: 3 quart

Serves: 6 – 8

Ingredients:

- Pumpkin (solid pack) = 1 can of 15 ounce (420 grams)
- Milk (evaporated) = 1 can of 12 ounces (360 ml)
- Sugar = ¾ Cup (150 grams)
- Biscuit mix or baking mix = ½ Cup (60 grams)

- Eggs (beaten) = 2
- Butter (melted) = 2 tablespoons (28 grams)
- Pumpkin pie spice = 2 ½ teaspoons (4.25 grams)
- Vanilla Extract = 2 teaspoons (10 ml)
- Whipped Cream as topping (optional)

Let's Cook:

1. Take a large bowl; Combine all the ingredients except whipped cream.
2. Take out your slow cooker and transfer the mixture into this.
3. Close the lid, switch the cooker on and let it cook on low heat setting for 6 – 7 hours or until the thermometer reads 160°C (320 ° F).
4. Once the slow cooker cooking cycle is finished, open it and transfer the pumpkin pie pudding to serving bowls.
5. Top with whipped cream. The delicious dessert is absolutely ready to be served.

2. Fudgy Brownie with strawberry

Completing dinner with a sweet note is always good to keep your mood up. However, you might be worrying about the number calories the dessert will add to your diet. Stop worrying now, because this chocolaty brownie has lesser calorie than other chocolate based desserts. The secret is applesauce which adds sweetness to the dish and also keeps the brownie moist. It uses very little amount of sugar. You can skip the sugar totally, if you wish. The deliciousness of the dish won't reduce. So, isn't that enough reason to try this dessert recipe? It is, for sure.

Preparation Time: 15 minutes

Cooking Time: 2 ½ - 3 hours

Stand-by Time: 30 minutes

Recommended Slow Cooker size: 6 quart

Serves: 10

Ingredients:

- Butter = ¼ Cup (56 grams)
- Chocolate (unsweetened) = 2 ounces (56 grams)
- Egg product (refrigerated or frozen, thawed) = ½ Cup (114 grams) or Beaten eggs = 2
- Sugar = ½ Cup (100 grams)
- Strawberry (seedless, sugar free) or Red strawberry Jam = 1/3 Cup (110 grams)
- Applesauce (unsweetened) = ¼ Cup (60 grams)
- Vanilla = 1 teaspoon (5 ml)
- All purpose flour = ¾ Cup (98 grams)

- Baking Powder = ¼ teaspoon (1 gram)
- Salt = ¼ teaspoon (1.2 grams)
- Warm Water = 1 Cup (235 ml)
- Dessert topping (light, frozen, thawed, whipped) = ¾ Cup (60 grams)
- Fresh Strawberries (sliced or whole) = 3 Cups (375 grams)
- Non stick Cooking spray
- Heavy foil

Let's Cook:

1. Take a 1 quart casserole or soufflé dish and lightly coat it with the non stick cooking spray. Cut an 18x12 inch heavy foil into half lengthwise. Fold each foil piece into one - thirds again lengthwise. Crisscross the two folded strips and place the casserole at the center of the crisscrossed foil. Keep it aside like that for now.
2. Now it's time to prepare the batter. Take a medium sauce pan; melt the butter and chocolate in it over low flame. Remove it from the heat.
3. Stir in beaten eggs or egg product to this. Now add sugar, jam, vanilla and applesauce. Beat the mixture with a spoon until smooth batter is achieved.
4. Now stir in flour, salt and baking powder. Again mix well. There should be no lumps.
5. Now pour this batter into the prepared soufflé dish or casserole. Cover it tightly with heavy foil.
6. Take out the slow cooker. Pour the warm water into this. Place the casserole or soufflé dish into the cooker by holding the ends of the foil strips. Leave the strips under the dish.

7. Close the lid, switch the cooker on and let it cook on high heat setting for 2 ½ - 3 hours or until the thermometer reads 170°C (338 ° F).
8. Once the cooking cycle ends, open the lid and take out the dish from the cooker by holding the ends of the foil strips. Turn the cooker off now.
9. Let it cool for 30 minutes on a wire rack.
10. Cut the brownie into serving size pieces. Top each brownie pieces with dessert topping and fresh strawberries.
11. Serve it and enjoy the yummy dessert.

3. Crust less Lemon Cheesecake

Do you always want to jump on to dessert after finishing dinner and also bother about the calorie intake? Don't worry at all and don't just be confused; Opt for such desserts that are tasty as well as healthy and so will not make you feel guilty for consuming more calories. Here is such a healthy, flavorful and zesty dessert recipe that can be good addition to your dessert menu. You will love this lemon cheesecake recipe once you prepare this by your own. Have it and you will feel heavenly pleasure.

Preparation Time: 20 minutes

Cooking Time: 2 – 3 hours

Chilling Time: 4 – 24 hours

Recommended Slow Cooker size: 3 ½ - 5 Quart

Serves: 8

Ingredients:

- Cream Cheese (softened) = 12 ounces (336 grams)
- Sugar = ½ Cup (100 grams)
- Lemon Juice = 2 tablespoons (30 ml)
- All purpose flour = 1 tablespoon (8 grams)
- Vanilla = ½ teaspoon (2.5 ml)
- Sour cream = ½ Cup (120 grams)
- Eggs (lightly beaten) = 3
- Lemon peel (finely shredded) = 2 teaspoons (10 grams)
- Warm Water = 1 Cup (235 ml)
- Fresh Raspberries (optional)
- Fresh mint (optional)

- Non stick cooking spray
- Heavy foil

Let's Cook:

1. Take a 1 quart casserole or soufflé dish and lightly coat it with the non stick cooking spray. Cut an 18 x 12 inch heavy foil into half lengthwise. Fold each foil piece into one - thirds again lengthwise. Crisscross the two folded strips and place the casserole at the center of the crisscrossed foils. Keep it aside like that for now.
2. Now it's time to prepare the batter. Take a large bowl; Combine Cream cheese, sugar, flour, lemon juice, and vanilla. Mix all well with an electric mixer on medium speed. Make sure there are no lumps.
3. Now stir in sour cream and again beat to mix well.
4. Add eggs and mix on low speed. Lastly add the lemon peel.
5. Now pour this batter into the prepared soufflé dish or casserole. Cover it tightly with heavy foil.
6. Take out the slow cooker. Pour the warm water into this. Place the casserole or soufflé dish into the cooker by holding the ends of the foil strips. Leave the strips under the dish.
7. Close the lid, switch the cooker on and let it cook on high heat setting for 2 ¼ - 2 ¾ hours or until the center of the cake is fixed. You can check by inserting a toothpick. If it comes out clean then the cake is done.
8. Once the cooker cycle ends, open the lid and take out the dish from the cooker by holding the ends of the foil strips. Turn the cooker off now.
9. Discard the foil. Let it cool on wire rack for few minutes. Cover and refrigerate it for 4 - 24 hours.

10. Take out the chilled lemon cheesecake just before serving. Cut it into serving size pieces. If you wish, top it with fresh raspberries and / or fresh mint and serve.

4. Chocolate bread pudding

It is such a dessert recipe, that even a kid can cook. You might have had bread pudding before; however, this particular bread pudding has an extra twist. It has Mocha 'cream' sauce that redefines the taste of bread pudding and promises to satisfy you to the fullest. This chocolaty dessert can be perfect for ending a chilling winter evening meal. It keeps you warm and its flavor will last long in your mouth to give you a cozy and comfort feeling. Get the recipe now and try this for sure.

Preparation Time: 20 minutes

Cooking Time: 2 ½ hours

Stand-by Time: 30 minutes

Recommended Slow Cooker size: 3 ½ - 4 quart

Serves: 8

Ingredients:

- Milk (fat free) = 3 Cups (720 ml)
- Chocolate pieces (bittersweet or semisweet) = ¾ Cup (120 grams)
- Cocoa Powder (presweetened) = ¾ Cup (90 grams)
- Egg substitute or egg product (fresh or frozen, thawed) = ¾ Cup (170 grams) or Eggs (lightly beaten) = 3
- Chia Seeds = 3 tablespoons (30 grams)
- Multi-grain bread cubes (reduced-calorie, ½ inch, dried) = 5 Cups (280 grams)
- Mocha 'Cream' Sauce = 1 recipe
- Non stick cooking spray

Let's Cook:

1. Take out your slow cooker. Lightly coat the cooker pot with non stick cooking spray. Otherwise you can line the cooker pot with a disposable cooker liner and then apply the non stick cooking spray on the liner. Keep the cooker aside for now.
2. Heat the milk in a medium sauce pan over medium flame until warm enough, but don't allow it to boil. Remove from heat.
3. Add in the chocolate pieces and cocoa powder to the warm milk (no need to stir). Let it stand for 5 minutes. Now whisk it nicely until smooth enough. Again keep it aside and let it cool for 10 minutes.
4. Take a large bowl; Combine beaten eggs or the egg substitute, chia seeds and the milk - chocolate mixture. Mix well.
5. Drop the bread cubes gently into this mixture.
6. Transfer this whole thing to the prepared slow cooker.
7. Close the lid, switch the cooker on and let it cook on low heat setting for 2 ½ hours or until a toothpick or knife inserted into the pudding, comes out clean. The mixture should puff up.
8. Turn the cooker off now.
9. Remove the liner and keep the whole thing on wire rack. Let it cool uncovered for 30 minutes. Pudding should start to fall as it cools down.
10. Spoon the warm pudding into dessert dishes. Pour some Mocha 'cream' sauce over it and serve.

5. Spicy Fruit Compote

Fruit compote is a perfect European dessert item that goes after a perfect summer lunch or dinner. It can be served warm or chilled. You can be flexible with the fruits. In fact you can add any fruit of your choice. You can also add spices of your choice. It is undoubtedly a very healthy and hearty dessert that anyone can enjoy at any time. You can top it with scoopful of ice cream or cinnamon or vanilla sugar or anything else that you feel would go well with it. The recipe below will explain how much easy it is to make. Just give it a try.

Preparation Time: 15 minutes

Cooking Time: 6 – 8 hours

Recommended Slow Cooker size: 3 ½ - 4 quart

Serves: 10

Ingredients:

- Pears (medium, peeled, cored, cubed) = 3
- Pineapple chunks (canned, undrained) = 1 can of 15 ½ ounces (435 grams)
- Apricots (dried, quartered) = 1 Cup (190 grams)
- Orange Juice Concentrate (frozen) = 3 tablespoons (45 ml)
- Brown Sugar (packed) = 2 tablespoons (22 grams)
- Quick cooking Tapioca = 1 tablespoon (11 grams)
- Fresh ginger (grated) = 1 teaspoon (1 gram) or Ginger (ground) = ½ teaspoon (1 gram)
- Pitted dark sweet cherries (frozen, unsweetened) = 2 Cups (450 grams)
- Coconut (toasted, flaked) (optional)

- Pecans or Macadamia nuts (chopped, toasted) (optional)

Let's Cook:

1. Take out your slow cooker. Arrange pears, pineapple chunks, apricots, orange juice concentrate, tapioca, brown sugar and ginger (grated or ground) in this.
2. Close the lid, switch the cooker on and let it cook on low heat setting for 6 – 8 hours or on high heat setting for 3 – 4 hours.
3. At the end of the cycle, stir in the cherries.
4. The dessert is ready. Transfer spoonful of the dessert to the serving bowls, top with nuts and coconut flakes if you wish and serve.

6. Rice Pudding

Rice pudding is particularly famous in Asian countries. However, it is served as dessert worldwide. The perception or the adaption of this dessert is different depending on the geographical location where it is being cooked and served. The main ingredients are milk, rice and sugar. You can be flexible with the rest of the ingredients. As it is a sweetish dish, it will add up some extra calorie to your diet. But that's fine as long as you are not having this every day, although it is quite tough to ignore its temptation. Let's peek at the easy cooking recipe of this traditional Asian dessert.

Preparation Time: 10 minutes

Cooking Time: 2 – 3 hours

Recommended Slow Cooker size: 3 ½ - 4 quart

Serves: 12

Ingredients:

- Rice (cooked) = 4 Cups (630 grams)
- Evaporated Milk = 1 can of 12 ounce (360 ml)
- Milk = 1 Cup (240 ml)
- Sugar = 1/3 Cup (150 grams)
- Water = ¼ Cup (~ 60 ml)
- Mixture of raisins, cranberries (dried) and / or cherries (dried) = 1 Cup (160 grams)
- Butter (softened) = 3 tablespoons (42 grams)
- Vanilla or Vanilla bean paste = 1 tablespoon (15 grams)
- Cinnamon (ground) = 1 teaspoon (2.3 grams)
- Non stick Cooking spray

Let's Cook:

1. Take out your slow cooker, coat it lightly with the non stick cooking spray. Keep it aside for now.
2. Take a large bowl; Combine cooked rice, milk, sugar, evaporated milk and water. Mix well.
3. Stir in raisins, softened butter, vanilla and cinnamon.
4. Transfer this mixture to the prepared slow cooker.
5. Close the lid, switch the cooker on and let it cook on low heat setting for 2 – 3 hours.
6. Once the cooking cycle is finished, open the lid, transfer and divide the rice pudding onto the serving bowls.
7. The yummy rice pudding is served. Just relish it.

7. Chocolaty Walnut bread pudding

We are often advised to incorporate walnut into our diet. Because it has many health benefits like it has anti-cancer properties; it fights against heart disease, diabetes, reproductive issues in men etc; it helps in weight loss and it is anti-oxidant. So, wouldn't it be nice if we can include this nut into our dessert? That surely sounds great. So, here is another chocolate bread pudding that has walnut as its main ingredient. It is super easy to make. Let's see the recipe now.

Preparation Time: 20 minutes

Cooking Time: 2 ½ hours

Stand – by Time: 30 minutes

Recommended Slow Cooker size: 3 ½ - 4 quart

Serves: 8

Ingredients:

- Walnuts (chopped) = ½ Cup (60 grams)
- Milk = 3 Cups (720 ml)
- Chocolate pieces (semisweet) = ¾ Cup (90 grams)
- Cocoa Powder (presweetened) = ¾ Cup (90 grams)
- Eggs (lightly beaten) = 3
- Hawaiian Sweet bread or Cinnamon – swirl bread (cubed, dried, no raisins) = 5 Cups (280 grams)
- Coffee Cream sauce = 1 recipe
- No stick cooking spray

Let's Cook:

1. Take out your slow cooker, coat it lightly with the non stick cooking spray. Keep it aside.
2. Take a medium sauce pan; Heat the milk in it over medium flame until warm enough, but don't allow it to boil. Remove from heat.
3. Add in the chocolate pieces and cocoa powder to the warm milk (no need to stir). Let it stand for 5 minutes. Now whisk it nicely until smooth enough. Again keep it aside and let it cool for 10 minutes.
4. Take a large mixing bowl; Mix the beaten eggs with the chocolate mixture in this.
5. Drop the bread cubes and walnuts gently into this mixture.
6. Pour this bread mixture to the prepared slow cooker.
7. Close the lid, switch the cooker on and let it cook on low heat setting for 2 ½ hours or until a toothpick or knife inserted into the pudding comes out clean. The mixture should puff up by now.
8. Remove the liner and keep on wire rack. Let it cool uncovered for 30 minutes. Pudding should start to fall as it cools down.
9. Spoon the warm pudding into dessert dishes. Pour some Coffee cream sauce over it and serve.

8. Strawberry Cheesecake

Whenever you have party at home, consider preparing this creamy and yummy strawberry cheesecake as the dessert of the evening. Be assured that your effort is going to be appreciated. It is perfect for a special occasion. So, don't forget to make this on your partner's birthday or on your anniversary. You will surely have a blast with this. With a slow cooker handy, if you prepare this special dessert, you can even turn your simple, regular dinner into a romantic one. The cream cheese in this dish creates magic. Whoever will have this is bound to go mad over this mouth watering dessert. So, what are you waiting for? Try it right away.

Preparation Time: 15 minutes

Cooking Time: 5 hours

Stand- by time: 45 minutes – 1 hour

Chilling Time: 2 – 3 hours

Recommended Slow Cooker size: 6 quart

Serves: 2

Ingredients:

- Whole Graham Crackers = 4
- Butter = 1 tablespoon (14 grams)
- Cream Cheese = 1 package of 8 ounce (224 grams)
- Egg = 1
- Honey = 1 tablespoon (18 grams)
- Strawberry Jam = 2 tablespoons (40 grams)
- Salt = ¼ teaspoon (1.2 grams)
- Fresh Strawberries (sliced, for topping)

- Water = 2 Cups (470 ml)

Let's Cook:

1. You need a food processor. Put the whole graham crackers in this and crush it completely. Add in butter and again mix until blended well.
2. You need 2 ramekins. Divide the cracker mixture into two halves. Press this mixture at the bottom of each of the ramekins.
3. In the same food processor make the batter now. Put cream cheese, honey, egg, salt and jam in this. Whisk until you get smooth batter. Divide the batter evenly into two portions and pour into the ramekins. Scrape down the food processor bowl to take out all the batter if needed.
4. Pour water into the slow cooker. Place both the ramekins in the cooker.
5. Close the lid, switch the cooker on and let it cook on low heat setting for 1 ½ – 2 hours or until the cheesecake is fully set.
6. Once the cycle is finished, turn the cooker off and open the lid. Leave the ramekins in the cooker for 45 to 60 minutes to allow it to cool. After that take them out.
7. Let them chill in refrigerator for 2 – 3 hours at least, take out, top with fresh strawberries and then serve.

9. Peach Cobbler

Cobbler can be of many types. It is mainly a baked dish popular in US and UK. Both US and UK version of cobbler is different from each other. Us cobbler version is thick-crusted pie with any fruit or fruit mixture filling and has biscuit batter as top layer; whereas UK cobbler version uses scone batter for the top layer. Out of many fruity cobblers 'Peach Cobbler' is a very famous one. If you love baking then you will have fun making this dish in slow cooker. And if you are new to baking then also there is no reason to worry, because most of the efforts will be taken care of by your great slow cooker. So, try this for sure in any case and end your evening meal on a nice note.

Preparation Time: 20 minutes

Cooking Time: 3 hours

Recommended Slow Cooker size: 6 quart

Serves: 8

Ingredients:

- Peaches (fresh or frozen, peeled, sliced) = 4 Cups (900 grams)
- Sugar = ¼ Cup (50 grams) + ½ Cup (100 grams)
- Original Biscuit Mix = 1 Cup (120 grams)
- Milk = 1 Cup (240 ml)
- Whipped cream or Ice cream (any flavor of your choice)
- Non stick cooking spray

Let's Cook:

1. Take out your slow cooker, coat it lightly with the non stick cooking spray.
2. Take a large bowl; Combine sliced peaches and sugar (1/4 Cup / 50 grams) in this. Toss to mix them. Transfer this mixture to the slow cooker.
3. In another medium sized bowl, combine Biscuit mix, sugar (1/2 Cup / 100 grams) and milk. Whisk until blended well. Make sure there are no lumps. Pour this mixture over the peaches in the slow cooker.
4. Close the lid, switch the cooker on and let it cook on low heat setting for 3 hours or until the peaches are set well at the center.
5. Your Peach cobbler is ready. Take it out from cooker with spoon and serve by topping it with Ice cream. It is going to taste awesome for sure.

10. Slow cooked Chocolate Fondue

Do you want to escape on a chilling evening? What could be more exciting than having a melting pot of chocolate fondue? And for having this you don't need to rush to any restaurant. You can make and have it at the cozy corner of your home. A slow cooker, four ingredients and 15 minutes of preparation time are all that you need to prepare this elegant dessert at home. You can dip any fruit pieces you have at home in this melting chocolate, put it into your mouth and enjoy a special heavenly pleasure. The recipe for this great elegant dessert is right here. Have fun baking this yummy dessert.

Preparation Time: 15 minutes

Cooking Time: 1 hour

Recommended Slow Cooker size: 6 quart

Serves: 8

Ingredients:

- Dark baking Chocolate (finely chopped) = 1 bar of 8 oz (224 grams)
- Whipped Cream = ½ Cup (120 grams)
- Butter = ½ Cup (112 grams)
- Liqueur (coffee favored, Irish cream or amaretto) = 1 teaspoon (5 ml)
- Assorted fresh fruits (like strawberry etc), cookies or marshmallows

Let's Cook:

1. Take out your slow cooker and pour 2 cups of water into it.
2. You need two ramekins. Divide the chocolate, cream, butter and liqueur equally and put into each of the ramekins.
3. Place the ramekins in the slow cooker.
4. Close the lid, switch the cooker on and let it cook on low heat setting for 45 – 60 minutes or until the chocolate is melted fully.
5. Once the cycle is finished, let it sit for some time and then take out the ramekins from the slow cooker.
6. Stir the chocolate fondue well with spoon. Serve it with assorted fruits or marshmallows or cookies or anything else you think would go well with this dessert.

11. White Chocolate Bread Pudding

Got some leftover bread and some sweet white chocolate at home? You can turn them into a comfort dessert and treat yourself with a great sweet dish after dinner. Yes, you can make white chocolate bread pudding very easily if you have a slow cooker handy. Once you try this, it is going to be your favorite dessert and cooking this dessert is going to be your favorite pastime for sure. Let's now get the recipe and plan to make it.

Preparation Time: 10 minutes

Cooking Time: 3 ½ - 4 hours

Recommended Slow Cooker size: 3 – 4 quart

Serves: 8

Ingredients:

- French Bread Cubes = 6 cups (336 grams)
- White Chocolate baking bar (coarsely chopped) = 1 package of 6 oz (168 grams)
- Egg product (fat free) = 1 cup (228 grams)
- Warm Water = ¾ Cup (175 ml)
- Vanilla = 1 teaspoon (5 ml)
- Condensed milk (sweetened, not evaporated) = 1 can of 14 oz (420 ml)
- Non stick cooking spray

Let's Cook:

1. Take out your slow cooker, coat it lightly with the non stick cooking spray.
2. First place the French bread cubes at the bottom of the slow cooker. Scatter the chopped chocolate baking bar on this.
3. Take a small bowl; Combine egg product, vanilla and condensed milk. Mix well. Pour over bread cubes and chocolate baking bar pieces in the cooker.
4. Close the lid, switch the cooker on and let it cook on low heat setting for 3 ½ – 4 hours or until you insert a toothpick at the center of the pudding and it comes out clean.
5. Once the cycle is finished, cut and take out parts of the pudding with spoon from the cooker and serve.

12. Blackberry Cobbler with sweet cornbread

Here is another fruit cobbler recipe for you. And you will love it too. Blackberry cobbler is much loved dessert and famous worldwide for its attractive look and yummy taste. This particular blackberry cobbler has sweetness of cornbread and muffin. It also has flavor of cinnamon. And it tastes out of the world when clubbed with whipped cream and ice cream. So, it is a must try recipe. With a slow cooker handy it becomes very easier to bake. Prepare this dessert when you have special occasion. Forget about calorie intake for one evening and indulge in this tasty temptation.

Preparation Time: 10 minutes

Cooking Time: 2 hours

Recommended Slow Cooker size: 4 ½ quart

Serves: 8

Ingredients:

- Blackberries (frozen) = 1 bag of 16 oz (448 grams)
- All purpose flour = 1 tablespoon (8 grams)
- Sugar = ½ Cup (100 grams)
- Butter (melted) = ½ Cup (112 grams)
- Cornbread and muffin mix = 1 pouch of 6.5 oz (180 grams)
- Cinnamon (ground) = 1 teaspoon (2.3 grams)
- Whipped cream and / or Ice cream (as needed)
- Baking spray

Let's Cook:

1. Take out your slow cooker, coat it lightly with the baking spray.
2. Scatter the blackberries at the bottom of the slow cooker.
3. Sprinkle all purpose flour and sugar (3 tablespoons / 37.5 grams) over the blackberries in the cooker. Stir gently to coat the berries with flour and sugar.
4. Take a small bowl; Combine melted butter, remaining sugar, cornbread mix and cinnamon in this. Make dough out of this mixture. Spread the dough onto the sugar coated blackberries in the cooker.
5. Close the lid, switch the cooker on and let it cook on low heat setting for 2 – 3 hours or until top of the dough is set well and blackberries become saucy.
6. Once the baking cycle is finished, ladle some amount of cake out of the cooker and place on a serving bowl or plate. Top it with whipped cream and / or ice cream before serving.

13. Slow Cooker Apple Butter

Apple butter can be a good dessert item. You can serve it with cookies or biscuits or breads. You can use it in wide variety of ways. This is cooked by concentrating applesauce along with raw apples over a long cooking process in which the sugar content in the apple gets caramelized eventually by giving it deep brown color. It can be preserved for long because of its concentrated sugar content.
Utilize the versatile cooking appliance, the slow cooker and prepare this zesty dessert. Make this in good quantity and you can use this for dessert frequently. Isn't that amazing? It is, for sure. So, let's get the recipe now.

Preparation Time: 30 minutes

Cooking Time: 12 hours

Recommended Slow Cooker size: 6 quart

Serves: Depends on use

Ingredients:

- Granny Smith or Fuji or Honey crisp Apples or combination of all types (peeled, cored, sliced) = 6 ½ pounds (182 grams)
- Applesauce (unsweetened) = 50 ounces (1.4 kg)
- Sugar (granulated) = 1 cup (200 grams)
- Brown sugar = 1 Cup (170 grams)
- Apple juice = 1 ½ Cups (375 ml)
- Cinnamon (ground) = 1 tablespoon (2.3 grams)
- Cloves (ground) = ¼ teaspoon (0.5 gram)
- Salt = ¼ teaspoon (1.2 grams)
- Allspice (ground) or nutmeg (ground) = ½ teaspoon (1.1 grams)

- Vanilla extract = 1 tablespoon (5 ml)

Let's Cook:

1. Peel the apples, core them and cut into small chips.
2. Now put all the ingredients into the slow cooker. Stir to combine.
3. Close the lid, switch the cooker on and let it cook on low heat setting for 10 hours or overnight.
4. Once the cooking cycle is finished, open the lid and stir in the vanilla extract. Now take out some butter with spoon and taste.
5. Adjust the sugar and spices if needed.
6. Continue cooking uncovered for few couple of hours more until the liquid is minimized and the butter gets cooked a bit more and gets the deep brown color.
7. Turn the cooker off now.
8. Pour the butter into a sterilized container and refrigerate.
9. Take it out few minutes in advance, whenever you want to serve your dessert.

14. Peanut Chocolate candy

These peanut chocolate candies are perfect for holidays. In holidays, in general you get time off from work, however keep occupied with household work or are surrounded by family members, friends, guests etc. So, there will be less time for cooking. But it will be nice to serve desserts to the guests after meals. So, here is a tasty solution for this. With a slow cooker handy you can keep your crunchy and yummy peanut chocolate candy ready to be served. And you don't need to spend any time for it. All the efforts will be taken care of by the slow cooker. You can arrange the few ingredients it needs and just chill.

Preparation Time: 5 minutes

Cooking Time: 3 hours

Stand by Time: 20 minutes

Recommended Slow Cooker size: 4 quart

Serves: 15 - 20

Ingredients:

- Peanuts (dry-roasted, salted) = 2 pounds (908 grams)
- Sweet German Chocolate = 4 ounces / about 4 squares (112 grams)
- Semi sweet chocolate chips = 1 package of 12 ounce / about 2 Cups (336 grams)
- White almond bark = 2 ½ pounds (1.2 kg)
- Cup cake pan liners (as per needed)

Let's Cook:

1. Take out your slow cooker. Arrange the peanuts at the bottom of it.
2. Layer the sweet chocolates over the peanuts. Then scatter the semi-sweet chocolate chips over this. Lastly add the almond bark. No need to stir the mixture.
3. Close the lid, switch the cooker on and let it cook on low heat setting for 3 hours.
4. Once the cooking cycle is finished, stir the mixture using a wooden spoon. Take out about two spoons of the peanut chocolate candy and pour onto each the cup cake pan liners.
5. Allow the chocolate candy to cool at least for about 20 minutes and then remove the cupcake liners. You can also keep the liners as it is.
6. The crunchy and yummy peanut chocolate candy is ready to serve. Get praised for making the awesome dessert.

15. Pineapple Upside Down Cake

Pineapple upside down cake is a classic retro style dessert that can bring back childhood memories and give you an overall delightful supper. The buttery soft, rich, caramelized pineapples are the special attraction of this dessert that will win your heart over. And you will be happier to know that this can be made at home with much ease if you have a slow cooker. So, try this luscious dessert at any time to make your evening meal a special and completely satisfying one.

Preparation Time: 15 minutes

Cooking Time: 3 hours

Stand by time: 15 minutes

Recommended Slow Cooker size: 6 quart

Serves: 12

Ingredients:

- Brown Sugar (packed) = 1 Cup (170 grams)
- Butter (melted) = ¼ Cup (56 grams)
- Pineapple (sliced, drained, reserve the juice) = 1 can of 20 oz (560 grams)
- Maraschino Cherries (without stem, drained) = 10
- Yellow cake mix = 1 box
- Eggs = 2
- Vegetable oil
- Non stick cooking spray

Let's Cook:

1. Take out your slow cooker, coat it lightly with the non stick cooking spray.
2. Take a small bowl; Mix the brown sugar and butter (melted) nicely. Use food processor if needed. Spread this mixture at the bottom of the slow cooker.
3. Now place pineapple slices in a layer on the butter mixture in the cooker. Place one cherry at the center of each slice and also in the gap in between slices if you like.
4. Take the reserved pineapple juice in a cup and fill the remaining portion of the cup with water.
5. Prepare the batter as directed on the cake mix box. Only replace water with the diluted pineapple juice. Beat the eggs and mix in this batter. Pour this batter over the pineapple slices and cherries in the slow cooker.
6. Close the lid, switch the cooker on and let it cook on high heat setting for 2 ½ – 3 hours or until you insert a toothpick at the center of the cake and it comes out clean.
7. Turn the cooker off and open the lid. Take out the ceramic base along with the cake from the cooker and let it cool on a rack for about 15 minutes.
8. Now place a heatproof plate upside down on the ceramic base. Carefully turn the whole thing over. Remove the ceramic base. The cake rests on the plate with the pineapple and cherries decorating its top.
9. Cut it in pieces and serve.

16. Slow cooker Carrot Cake

It is probably the most conventional, traditional yet most popular dessert item. You won't be able to forget the taste and temptation of a slow cooker made carrot cake. Try this, have it and you will know. It is soft, moist and purely flavorful dish. The grated carrots give a nice texture and flavor to the cake. You can have this in any season and at any time. So, cook this all time favorite dessert at home and have blast.

Preparation Time: 45 minutes

Cooking Time: 2 ½ hours

Recommended Slow Cooker size: 3 quart

Serves: 12

Ingredients:

- Sugar = 1 Cup (200 grams)
- Eggs = 2
- Water = ¼ Cup (~ 60 ml)
- Vegetable oil = 1/3 Cup (75 grams)
- All purpose Flour = 1 ½ Cups (195 grams)
- Vanilla extract = 1 teaspoon (5 ml)
- Baking powder = 1 teaspoon (5 grams)
- Baking soda = ½ teaspoon (3.5 grams)
- Cinnamon (ground) = 1 teaspoon (2.3 grams)
- Carrots (grated, packed) = 1 Cup (90 grams)
- Whipped cream (for topping)
- Non-stick cooking spray.

Let's Cook:

1. Take out your slow cooker, coat it lightly with the non stick cooking spray.
2. Take a small bowl; Mix sugar, eggs, vegetable oil and water. Blend nicely.
3. Add flour, baking powder, baking soda, vanilla and ground cinnamon. Blend again nicely.
4. Stir in the grated carrots. Mix with hand until all the carrot pieces are distributed uniformly in the batter.
5. Pour the batter inside the greased crock pot. Let it spread evenly at the bottom of the pot.
6. Close the lid, switch the cooker on and let it cook on low heat setting for 2 – 3 hours. Check whether the cake is done, by inserting a toothpick at the center of it and see if it comes out clean.
7. Remove the ceramic base or the crock from the cooker and keep on a rack to cool for some time.
8. Cut pieces from it and place on the serving plates. Brush up your icing skill and decorate the cakes with whipped cream topping before serving.

17. Lemon – Poppy seed Cake

This cake is sweet, tangy, simple and luscious in true sense. The mouthwatering moist texture of this cake will surely win over your taste buds. Try this at home with your slow cooker and be overwhelmed to taste the outcome. Don't forget to nurture your frosting skill which will make the cake even more appealing in look and taste. Get the recipe and get ready to make this now.

Preparation Time: 20 minutes

Cooking Time: 2 hours

Stand-by time: 15 minutes

Recommended Slow Cooker size: 3 quart

Serves: 4

Ingredients:

- All purpose flour = 1 ¾ cups (228 grams)
- Yellow cornmeal = ½ Cup (83 grams)
- Baking powder = 1 teaspoon (5 grams)
- Baking soda = 1 teaspoon (7 grams)
- Kosher salt = ¼ teaspoon (1.2 grams)
- Butter (unsalted, at room temperature) = 12 tablespoons / 1 ½ sticks (168 grams)
- Sugar (granulated) = 1 ¼ Cups (250 grams) + 6 tablespoons (84 grams)
- Eggs = 2 large
- Sour cream = 1 Cup (240 grams)
- Pure vanilla extract = ½ teaspoon (2.5 ml)
- Lemon zest (grated) = 1 tablespoon (15 grams)

- Lemon juice = 2 tablespoons (30 ml)
- Poppy seeds = 1 teaspoon (2.8 grams)
- Confectioner's Sugar = 1 tablespoon (8 grams)
- Whipped cream (for topping)
- Cup cake pan liners (as needed)or Parchment Paper (for lining the cooker pot)

Let's Cook:

1. Take a mixing bowl; Combine flour, baking powder, baking soda, cornmeal and salt. Whisk nicely.
2. Mix the butter and 1 ¼ cups (250 grams) of granulated sugar with a mixer in medium-high speed. Make sure the mixture is smooth enough. Add the eggs and beat in the mixture.
3. Now add vanilla, lemon zest, sour cream and poppy seeds. Blend with the mixer. Reduce the mixer speed to low and slowly stir in the flour mixture. The cake batter is ready now.
4. Place the 15 inch piece of parchment paper at the bottom of the slow cooker. Pour the batter onto it. Alternatively you can use cup cake pan liners and pour two spoons of batter into each liner ad place them in the slow cooker.
5. Close the lid, switch the cooker on and let it cook on high heat setting for 2 hours or until a toothpick inserted at the center of the cake comes out clean.
6. In a small bowl, mix the lemon juice and remaining 6 tablespoons (84 grams) of granulated sugar. Add drizzles of this sweet juice over the cake.
7. Take the cake out by holding the sides of the parchment paper or just remove the whole crock with the cup cakes and place it on a rack for cooling. After about 15 minutes sprinkle the confectioner's sugar and spread the whipped cream on the cake before serving.

18. Sour Cream Cheesecake

Nobody can ignore the temptation of this slow cooker made silky smooth creamy cheesecake. It will just melt down, once in your mouth and will leave a strong, satisfying flavor that you will cherish for long. It's also super easy to cook at home. So, plan to make this when you expect guests at home. Your effort will be less and you will be praised for serving so delicious dessert. No point in waiting more. Let's peek at the recipe and try it.

Preparation Time: 20 minutes

Cooking Time: 2 hours

Stand-by Time: 2 hours

Chilling Time: 4 hours

Total Time: 8 hours 20 minutes

Recommended Slow Cooker size: 6 – 7 Quart

Serves: 6

Ingredients:

- Graham Cracker Crumbs = ¾ Cup (75 grams)
- Butter (unsalted, melted) = 2 ½ tablespoons (35 grams)
- Cinnamon (ground) = ¼ teaspoon (0.5 gram)
- Sugar = 2/3 Cup (120 grams) + 1 tablespoon (12.5 grams)
- Cream Cheese (at room temperature) = 12 ounces (336 grams)
- All purpose flour = 1 tablespoon (8 grams)
- Eggs = 2 large
- Almond extract (pure) = 1 teaspoon (5 ml)

- Sour cream = 1 Cup (240 grams)
- Salt

Let's Cook:

1. Take a medium bowl; Combine graham cracker crumbs, melted butter, ground cinnamon, sugar (1 tablespoon / 12.5 grams) and salt (a pinch) in this. Transfer this mixture to a deep bottom, flat springform pan.
2. Mix the cream cheese with the flour, sugar (2/3 Cup / 120 grams) and salt (1/4 teaspoon / 1.2 grams) in a mixer at medium-high speed for about 2 minutes or until smooth enough. Add the eggs and almond extract in this. Again blend at medium speed until well combined. Lastly add the sour cream and blend again until smooth enough. Pour this batter in the springform pan.
3. Now it's time to take out your slow cooker. Fill the cooker pot with water till ½ inch from bottom. Place a rack on this and let the springform pan sit over this containing the cheesecake batter. Now cover the cooker with triple layer of paper towels and then close the lid. Switch the cooker on and let it cook on high heat setting for 2 hours. Although it's tough, but please refrain yourself from peeking inside while the cooking cycle is on. It's important.
4. Once the cooking cycle is finished, turn the cooker off and let it cool for 1 hour.
5. Now open the lid, remove the paper towels, take out the cheesecake and keep it on a rack for 1 hour to allow it to come to room temperature.
6. Now cover the cheesecake with plastic wrap and refrigerate for 4 hours or until chilled.

7. Heat a thin, sharp knife by immersing in hot water; Let it dry. Now run the knife along the cheesecake edges carefully in order to release the cake from the pan. Lift the cheesecake and transfer to a plate.
8. Cut into 6 or 8 wedges, top with whipped cream if you desire and serve.

19. Apple Granola

A crunchy yet mouthwatering dessert will give your taste buds a break from regular and usual dessert dishes. While slow cooking, the apples get tender and get zesty treatment from the granola cereal. So, the outcome becomes exceptionally tempting. Apart from that, granola is packed with lots of nutrients. So, in the name of dessert you get a nutritious treat too. What more can you expect from a dessert? Deliciousness, nutrition and the utmost temptation, you get it all in this. Isn't that enough reason to try this dessert at home? It is. So, get the recipe and get ready to cook it.

Preparation Time: 10 minutes

Cooking Time: 6 hours

Recommended Slow Cooker size: 1 ½ quart

Serves: 4

Ingredients:

- Tart Apples (medium, peeled, sliced) = 4
- Granola cereal containing fruits and nuts = 2 Cups (240 grams)
- Honey = ¼ Cup (72 grams)
- Butter (melted) = 2 tablespoons (28 grams)
- Cinnamon (ground) = 1 teaspoon (2.3 grams)
- Nutmeg (ground) = ½ teaspoon (1.1 grams)
- Whipped topping (optional)

Let's Cook:

1. Take out your slow cooker. Arrange apples and cereal in this.
2. Take a small bowl; Mix honey, butter, nutmeg and cinnamon. Pour this mixture over the apple and cereal in the cooker. Mix everything well with a slotted spoon.
3. Close the lid, switch the cooker on and let it cook on low heat setting for 6 – 7 hours.
4. Once the cooking cycle is finished, open the lid, take the granola out of the cooker using a spoon and decorate with whipped topping, if you like, before serving.

20. Bananas Foster

Bananas are always welcomed. They are good in desserts as well. This one is special and really creative one. Bananas Foster was first made at a restaurant in New Orleans, Louisiana in 1950s (New Orleans was a big hub for importing bananas at that time). In this dessert, bananas are cooked with brown sugar, rum, cinnamon etc and served with ice cream. The flavors of rum, caramel, walnuts complement the yummy, slow cooked bananas and make this a complete classy and elegant dessert. Nobody can ignore the temptation of this dish once tasted. And when this yummy item is coupled with ice cream it becomes simply superb. It is also super easy to make. Try and see.

Preparation Time: 10 Minutes

Cooking Time: 2 Hours

Recommended Slow Cooker size: 1 ½ Quart

Serves: 5

Ingredients:

- Firm Bananas (medium) = 5
- Brown Sugar (packed) = 1 Cup (170 grams)
- Butter (melted) = ¼ Cup (56 grams)
- Rum = ¼ Cup (62 ml)
- Vanilla Extract = 1 teaspoon (5 ml)
- Cinnamon (ground) = ½ teaspoon (1.1 grams)
- Walnuts (chopped) = 1/3 Cup (40 grams)
- Coconut (flaked) = 1/3 Cup (33 grams)
- Ice cream (vanilla flavored) or pound cake (sliced)

Let's Cook:

1. First of all, cut the bananas in half lengthwise and then crosswise. Layer the cut banana pieces at the bottom of the slow cooker.
2. Take a bowl; Combine brown sugar, melted butter, vanilla extract, rum and ground cinnamon in this. Pour this mixture over the bananas in the cooker.
3. Close the lid, switch the cooker on and let it cook on low heat setting for 1 ½ hours.
4. Once the cooking cycle is finished, open the lid and sprinkle chopped walnuts and coconut flakes on the bananas foster. Again close the lid and continue to cook for another half an hour. Now the dish is ready.
5. Take it out with ladder and place on a serving plate. Top with ice cream or pound cake and serve. You can serve it warm or chilled. It tastes awesome in both ways.

21. Double Apple Cake

Are you looking for an extravagant apple dessert? We most probably have found it for you. The double apple cake is arguably the best apple dessert anyone can have. It can be enjoyed in all seasons and at any time and on any occasion. In this dessert, applesauce enhances the satisfying flavor of apple and moreover the spices (cinnamon, nutmeg etc) add more twist to the taste. No bite of this cake can go boring as it is stuffed with fresh and dried apples and drizzled with various decadent ingredients like brown sugar, vanilla extract, buttermilk and what not. All of these sound interesting for sure. Let's try this recipe now and taste it to verify its lusciousness.

Preparation Time: 20 Minutes

Cooking Time: 1 ½ Hours

Recommended Slow Cooker size: 5 Quart

Serves: 8

Ingredients:

- All purpose flour = 1 ½ Cups or 6.75 ounces (190 grams)
- Dark Brown Sugar (packed) = 1/3 Cup (57 grams)
- Baking Soda = 1 teaspoon (7 grams)
- Cinnamon (ground) = 1 ½ teaspoons (3.5 grams)
- Baking powder = ½ teaspoon (2.5 grams)
- Salt = ¼ teaspoon (1.2 grams)
- Nutmeg (ground) = ¼ teaspoon (0.5 gram)
- Cloves (ground) = 1/8 teaspoon (0.25 grams)
- Applesauce (unsweetened) = 1 Cup (244 grams)
- Buttermilk (low fat) = 1/3 Cup (80 ml)

- Butter (melted) = ¼ Cup (56 grams)
- Vanilla extract = 1 tablespoon (15 ml)
- Egg = 1 large
- Apples (dried, sliced, coarsely chopped) = 1 Cup (120 grams)
- Powdered sugar (optional) = 1 teaspoon (3.3 grams)
- Parchment paper (as cooker liner)
- Non stick cooking spray

Let's Cook:

1. Take out your slow cooker, coat it lightly with the non stick cooking spray.
2. Now line the bottom of the cooker with parchment paper. Cut 2 strips (30 inch long) of parchment paper and place them in X pattern over the cooker liner. Coat the parchment paper with non stick cooking spray as well. The slow cooker is all geared up for cooking. Keep it aside.
3. Take a medium bowl; Combine flour, baking powder, baking soda, brown sugar, cinnamon, nutmeg, cloves and salt in this. Stir well.
4. In another small bowl, mix applesauce with buttermilk, melted butter, vanilla and egg. Add this mixture to the flour mixture. Whisk until smooth enough. Now stir in the dried apples.
5. Pour this prepared batter into the slow cooker and spread it evenly in one layer.
6. Close the lid, switch the cooker on and let it cook on high heat setting for 1 – 1 ½ hours or until a toothpick inserted at the center of the cake comes out clean.
7. Once the cooking cycle is finished, open the lid and cut the Double apple cake into wedges. Sprinkle powdered sugar on this, if you like and serve warm.

22. Spicy Poached Pear

Poached pears with touch of spices are simple, delicious yet so elegant and satisfying. Slow cooking makes the pears almost ready to melt and the wine makes it so exotic that you will cherish its aftertaste for long. Anjou pears (European pears) are the best for this recipe, because they are naturally aromatic and have pleasant sweetish taste with a little citrus touch. If you serve these poached pears as dessert for your party next time, be assured that your guests will be delighted to taste such a pleasantly different dish. So, what are you waiting for? Plan to cook this for your next indoor party and enjoy to the fullest. The recipe is right below here.

Preparation Time: 10 Minutes

Cooking Time: 3 – 4 Hours

Recommended Slow Cooker size: 5 Quart

Serves: 6

Ingredients:

- Firm Ripe Anjou Pears (peeled) = 6
- Vino Santo or any other sweet dessert wine of your choice = 1 bottle of 16 oz (500 ml)
- Sugar = ½ Cup (100 grams)
- Orange juice (fresh) = 1/3 Cup (80 ml)
- Vanilla bean (3 inch, split lengthwise) = 1
- Juniper berries = ¼ teaspoon (1.2 grams)
- Cinnamon Stick (3 inch) = 1
- Crème Fraiche (optional) = 6 tablespoons (90 grams)
- Ground cinnamon (optional)

Let's Cook:

1. Firstly remove cores from ends of pears (leave stem end as it is). To make it sit flat, cut about ¼ inch from its base if needed. Do it for each pear.
2. Pour wine, sugar and fresh orange juice into the slow cooker. Keep stirring with a spoon until sugar dissolves completely.
3. Remove seeds from vanilla bean. Stir in the seeds and the bean to the wine mixture in the cooker.
4. Now add juniper berries and cinnamon stick to the cooker. Let the pears sit properly in the mixture.
5. Close the lid, switch the cooker on and let it cook on high heat setting for 3 hours or until the pears are tender enough.
6. Once the cooking cycle is finished, remove the pears from the cooker and place on serving plates (each on one plate). You can keep them whole as it is or can cut into halves.
7. Now it's time to process the cooking liquid left in the cooker. Transfer the liquid to a medium saucepan through a sieve. Discard the solids. Bring it to boil and keep boiling for about 20 minutes or until the liquid reduces to 1 cup measure. The sauce is ready now.
8. Pour this sauce evenly on each poaches pears. The spicy sauce will add nice flavor and taste to the poached pears.
9. Top each pear with Crème Fraiche and sprinkle cinnamon before serving. Garnishing is fully optional. Perform this step only if you like it. The spicy poached pears will taste heavenly always.

23. Mixed Berry Compote (over Angel food Cake)

Berries are always loved and they are delectably tasty. So, any dessert made with mixture of all the berries (Blueberry, Blackberry and Raspberry) is bound to be super tasty. Mixed berry compote is really an extremely flavorful and utmost enchanting dessert item. You can use this compote as sauce over Angel Food cake and thus prepare a new, creative, toothsome dessert. This is very easy to prepare and needs very few easy to find ingredients. Let's look at the recipe now and try to make this awesome dessert at home.

Preparation Time: 5 Minutes

Cooking Time: 3 Hours 15 minutes

Recommended Slow Cooker size: 5 Quart

Serves: 8

Ingredients:

- Blueberries = 2 Cups (290 grams)
- Blackberries = 2 Cups (290 grams)
- Raspberries = 2 Cups (290 grams)
- Orange juice = 1 Cup (240 ml)
- Sugar = ½ Cup (100 grams)
- Cornstarch = 3 tablespoons (31 grams)
- Water = 6 tablespoons (~ 90 ml)
- Angel Food cake (cut into 8 thin slices) = 1 of 8 ounces (224 grams)
- Non stick cooking spray

Let's Cook:

1. Take out your slow cooker, coat it lightly with the non stick cooking spray.
2. Arrange all the berries, orange juice and sugar at the bottom of the cooker.
3. Close the lid, switch the cooker on and let it cook on high heat setting for 3 hours. Open the lid.
4. In a small bowl, combine cornstarch and water. Mix well until smooth. Pour this cornstarch mixture into the slow cooker on the cooked berry mixture.
5. Close the lid again and let it cook on high heat setting for 15 minutes or until the sauce thickens.
6. The mixed berry compote is ready. Serve it by pouring over the angel food cake slices.

24. Cinnamon – raisin Bread Pudding

If you prefer having dessert after evening meal, however feel that cooking the dessert is an extra burden for your busy schedule, then consider hassle free slow cooker process to prepare desserts. You will simply love to make them over and over again. So, here is a lovely dessert for you, the superb Cinnamon-raisin bread pudding. They are awesome winter dessert and can be made very easily. It needs just handful of ingredients and 10 minutes of preparation. Rest will be done by slow cooker as it will cook it with steaming without expecting any attention from your side. So, try this today and have loads of fun while having this.

Preparation Time: 10 Minutes

Cooking Time: 2 Hours

Stand-by Time: 30 Minutes

Recommended Slow Cooker size: 4 Quart

Serves: 6

Ingredients:

- Eggs = 3 large
- Light Brown sugar (packed) = ½ Cup (85 grams)
- Nutmeg (ground) = ½ teaspoon (1.1 grams)
- Milk = 1 Cup (240 ml)
- Whipping cream = 1 Cup (240 grams)
- Vanilla extract = 1 teaspoon (5 ml)
- Butter (melted) = ¼ Cup (56 grams)
- Cinnamon-raisin bread loafs (cut into 1 inch cubes) = 1 pound (454 grams)

- Cinnamon chips (if available) or Butterscotch Chips = ½ Cup (~ 65 grams)
- Pecans (chopped, toasted) = ½ Cup (65 grams)
- Whipped cream (sweetened, optional)
- Non stick cooking spray.

Let's Cook:

1. Take a large bowl; Whisk together eggs, light brown sugar and ground nutmeg in this. Stir in milk, whipping cream, vanilla and melted butter.
2. Now add the bread cubes and keep stirring gently until all the bread cubes are soaked in the mixture. Stir in butterscotch chips and pecans.
3. Now take out your slow cooker, coat it lightly with the non stick cooking spray.
4. Pour the mixture into the greased slow cooker carefully.
5. Close the lid, switch the cooker on and let it cook on low heat setting for 2 hours or until a toothpick inserted at the center of the pudding comes out clean.
6. Once the cooking cycle is finished, open the lid and take out the ceramic base from the cooker containing the pudding. Let it cool down for about 30 minutes.
7. Serve the cinnamon-raiding bread pudding warm. Top it with whipped cream if you wish.

25. Chocolate Brownie Sundaes

Brownie sundaes are both visibly and taste wise yummy and rich. Ignoring its temptation is next to impossible. It is a classic dessert that is popular with everyone. You can never go wrong with this. You will feel heavenly while adoring the layers of gooey, warm brownie coupled with chilling vanilla ice cream. This adds a 'feel good' factor to your evening meal. Forget about the calorie intake once in a while and indulge this luxurious, classy dessert. And you don't need to rush to restaurant to have this. With a fabulous slow cooker handy you can prepare this at home quite effortlessly and enjoy your leisure time. So, take a look at the recipe and plan to cook this yummy, rich dessert soon.

Preparation Time: 5 Minutes

Cooking Time: 4 Hours

Stand-by Time: 30 Minutes

Recommended Slow Cooker size: 3 Quart

Serves: 6 – 8

Ingredients:

- Dark chocolate fudge brownie mix = 1 package of 19.8 ounce (554 grams)
- Butter (melted) = ¾ Cup (168 grams)
- Sugar = ½ Cup (100 grams)
- Eggs (lightly beaten) = 6 large
- Vanilla Ice cream = 1 pint (~ 500 ml)
- Non stick cooking spray

Let's Cook:

1. Take out your slow cooker, coat it lightly with the non stick cooking spray.
2. Take a large bowl; Combine brownie mix, melted butter, sugar and eggs in this.
3. Pour this mixture into the greased slow cooker pot.
4. Close the lid, switch the cooker on and let it cook on low heat setting for 4 hours or until the edges of the brownie easily pulls away from the cooker pot, but the center is still soft.
5. Switch the cooker off, let it stand for 30 minutes and then take out the brownie with spoon.
6. Serve Chocolate Brownie Sundae with vanilla Ice cream. You will get a restaurant like feel at home while having this. It's the magic of slow cooker.

26. Pecan Pie

Pecan pie is a Southern American dessert item that is adored worldwide. Pecan is a type of nut that is highly nutritious. If you avoid desserts because you think they incorporate unnecessary fats in your diet and are totally unhealthy, then you can make this pecan pie which is a healthy one. Pecan is good source of Manganese, protein, unsaturated fats, omega – 6 fatty acids etc. It also has cholesterol reducing properties. What more one can ask from a tasty and healthy dessert? You can have this dessert frequently and being worry free. Slow cooking makes this dessert more charming and toothsome. So, make this dessert effortlessly with slow cooker and enjoy your dessert time.

Preparation Time: 5 Minutes

Cooking Time: 4 Hours

Stand-by Time: 30 Minutes

Recommended Slow Cooker size: 4 Quart

Serves: 16

Ingredients:

- Honey = ½ Cup (144 grams) if mild sweetness is preferred or ¾ Cup (216 grams) if moderate sweetness is preferred
- Egg white (whipped with a fork) from 3 eggs
- Pecans (diced) = 2 cups (250 grams)
- Vanilla Extract = 4 teaspoons (20 ml)
- Cinnamon = 1 teaspoon (2.3 grams)
- Cornstarch or white whole wheat flour = 3 tablespoons (30 grams)
- Pie crust (readily available, unbaked) = 1

- Oil
- Parchment paper

Let's Cook:

1. Take out your slow cooker, coat it lightly with oil.
2. Line the cooker bottom with parchment paper. Let it fit properly so that removing the pie after cooking becomes easy.
3. Take a large bowl, mix all the ingredients in this and pour into the unbaked pie crust. Place the whole thing into the slow cooker carefully.
4. Close the lid, switch the cooker on and let it cook on low heat setting for 3 hours.
5. Open the lid carefully by not allowing any water droplet to drip onto the pie. Continue to cook uncovered for one more hour.
6. Once the cooking cycle is finished, run a knife alongside the pie to gently separate it from the side of the pot and then remove the whole pie carefully by holding the edges of the parchment paper. Place it on a rack and let it cool for at least 30 minutes.
7. Cut the pecan pie into wedges and serve.

27. Rich Hot Fudge Cake

Here is a totally fun recipe for today's dessert. true. Making hot fudge cake in slow cooker is There is no skill required to bake this cake. Ju the handful of ingredients, spend 15 minutes for arrang… things and slow cooker will do the rest. You just wait to taste the awesome outcome. Once you cook this you will fall in love with the crock pot and will praise yourself for having bought this and will keep preparing this dessert whenever you get a chance. So, just get the recipe here in details and get ready to cook the rich hot fudge cake tonight.

Preparation Time: 15 Minutes

Cooking Time: 2 ½ Hours

Stand-by Time: 30 Minutes

Recommended Slow Cooker size: 4 – 5 Quart

Serves: 6

Ingredients:

- All purpose flour = 1 Cup (130 grams)
- Sugar = ½ Cup (100 grams)
- Cocoa Powder = 6 tablespoons (45 grams)
- Baking Powder = 2 teaspoons (10 grams)
- Salt = ½ teaspoon (2.5 grams)
- Milk = ½ Cup (120 ml)
- Oil = 2 tablespoons (28 grams)
- Vanilla Extract = 1 teaspoon (5 ml)
- Chopped Nuts (optional) = ½ Cup (60 grams)

- Brown Sugar (packed) = ¾ Cup (128 grams)
- Hot water = 1 ½ Cups (353 ml)
- Non Stick Cooking Spray
- Vanilla Ice cream (scoops, as needed)

Let's Cook:

1. Take out your slow cooker, coat it lightly with the non stick cooking spray.
2. Take a medium bowl; sift the flour, sugar cocoa powder (2 tablespoons / 15 grams), salt and baking powder in this. Mix well.
3. Stir in milk, vanilla extract and oil in the mixture. Stir well until all are combined. Scatter the chopped nuts on this mixture.
4. Pour the batter evenly into the slow cooker.
5. In another bowl, mix brown sugar and remaining cocoa powder. Add hot water in this and stir well. Pour this mixture over the batter in the cooker. No need to stir.
6. Close the lid, switch the cooker on and let it cook on high heat setting for 2 ½ hours. Insert a toothpick at the center; if it comes out clean, then the cake is done. The upper layer is the cake and bottom layer is the hot fudge sauce.
7. Once the cooking cycle is finished, open the lid and let it cool down for about half an hour.
8. Slice up the rich hot fudge cake, place on a serving plate and then take spoonful of fudge sauce to pour over the cake. Now couple this with scoopful of vanilla ice cream and serve. No other dessert in the world can compete with this one. Let one spoonful of this dessert enter your mouth and feel the heavenly pleasure.

28. Pina Colada Lava Cake

Pina Colada is basically a famous cocktail made up of rum, pineapple juice and cream of coconut. It is national drink of Puerto Rico since 1978. The combination of Pina colada ingredients seems to be very tempting. What if, these ingredients are used to bake a yummy cake? The cake would definitely turn out to be extremely decadent. So, here we brought a slow cooker made Pina Colada Lava cake recipe. We excused the rum in this and added vanilla flavor to this apart from the essence of pineapple. You will be proud of yourself once you make this tropical, exotic dessert. The recipe is right here. Go through it and cook this cake.

Preparation Time: 15 minutes

Cooking Time: 3 – 4 Hours

Recommended Slow Cooker size: 3 – 4 Quart

Serves: 6

Ingredients:

- Vanilla = 1 teaspoon (5 ml)
- Flour = 1 Cup (130 grams)
- Baking Powder = 1 ½ teaspoons (7.5 grams)
- Cream of coconut = 1 can of 14 oz (420 ml)
- Pineapple (crushed, drained, juice reserved) = 1 can of 16 oz (448 grams)
- Vegetable or Canola Oil = 2 tablespoons (28 grams)
- Coconut (shredded) = 1 Cup (100 grams)
- Coconut milk = 1 Cup (250 ml)
- Vanilla Ice cream

Let's Cook:

1. Spread the crushed pineapples at the bottom of the slow cooker evenly.
2. Take a medium bowl; Combine flour, baking powder, vanilla extract, cream of coconut (1/3 Cup / 80 ml), reserved pineapple juice (2/3 Cup / 144 ml), Shredded coconut (1/2 Cup / 50 grams) and vegetable oil in this. Stir nicely until mixed well. Spread this mixture over the pineapples in the slow cooker.
3. In a pan, stir in coconut milk and cream of coconut and bring it boil over medium heat. Pour this boiling mixture on top of the batter in the cooker. No need to stir.
4. Close the lid, switch the cooker on and let it cook on low heat setting for 3 – 4 hours or on high for 2 – 3 hours.
5. Now place the remaining shredded coconut on a cookie sheet. Toast it in an oven for couple of minutes.
6. Once the cooking cycle is finished, take out the cake from the cooker and transfer to serving bowls. Top with vanilla ice cream and toasted coconuts before serving.

29. Marshmallow Brownie

Marshmallow is a sweet candy that contains sugar and is molded into small cylindrical shape and is generally coated with cornstarch. They are good dessert ingredient. Few marshmallow recipes need egg and others do not. No doubt that brownie made of these sweet marshmallows will be utmost tasty. And in this slow cooker version of Marshmallow brownie the sugar candies are melted and blended with chocolates. The interesting part is that making this super yummy, rich and elegant dessert is almost effortless. Get the recipe, arrange the ingredients and switch on the slow cooker. That much is your duty as a cook and you will be gifted with aromatic, zesty outcome. Try it now.

Preparation Time: 15 Minutes

Cooking Time: 1 ½ - 2 Hours

Stand-by Time: 30 Minutes

Recommended Slow Cooker size: 3 Quart

Serves: 6

Ingredients:

- Butter = 4.5 oz (125 grams)
- Dark Chocolate (broken into small pieces) = 4.5 oz (125 grams)
- Eggs = 2 medium
- Caster sugar = 5 ½ oz (150 grams)
- Cocoa Powder = 0.7 oz (20 grams)
- Plain flour = 2.2 oz (60 grams)
- Large Marshmallow (cut into half) = 10
- Non stick cooking spray

- Parchment paper (for lining the cooker)

Let's Cook:

1. Take out your slow cooker, coat it lightly with the non stick cooking spray.
2. Line the cooker pot with the parchment paper.
3. Firstly chop the butter and dark chocolates into small pieces and place in a small bowl. Microwave this for couple minutes on high heat setting. Take it out and allow cooling.
4. Mix the caster sugar and eggs in an electric mixture until thick and smooth.
5. Pour the cooled chocolate mixture into the egg and sugar mixture. Let it sit for few minutes so that they mix together slowly and completely.
6. Sieve the cocoa powder and flour into the above mixture. Allow all the ingredients to mix completely. Give a gentle stir, not vigorous.
7. Lastly stir in the Marshmallow pieces. Now the batter for the brownie is ready.
8. Pour the batter into the greased cooker.
9. Close the lid, switch the cooker on and let it cook on high heat setting for 1 ½ – 2 hours or until a toothpick inserted at the center comes out clean.
10. Once the cooking cycle is finished, open the lid (the yummy look of the brownie would already start tempting you, but hold on) and let it cool completely (it will take at least 30 minutes). Take the brownie out of the slow cooker by holding the sides of the parchment paper.
11. It is now ready to serve. Cut the Marshmallow brownie into wedges and start eating straight away.

30. Almond and Plum Cake

Here is an autumn special dessert recipe. It uses plums (easily available at the end of summer) and almonds. It tastes best if eaten fresh. It stays delightfully moist, toothsome and flavorful. When this cake is topped with warm damson jam, chopped fresh plums and is sprinkled with crunchy caster sugar, it gets more delicious. Enjoy the effortless baking of this cake with slow cooker and have great dessert time.

Preparation Time: 10 Minutes

Cooking Time: 1 – 2 Hours

Stand-by Time: 30 Minutes

Recommended Slow Cooker size: 4 – 5 Quart

Serves: 6

Ingredients:

- Butter = 6 oz (170 grams)
- Golden Caster Sugar = 6.5 oz (180 grams)
- Self raising flour = 5 ½ oz (150 grams)
- Eggs = 3 medium
- Almond extract = 1 teaspoon (5 ml)
- Ground Almonds = 2 ½ oz (70 grams)
- Baking powder = ½ teaspoon (2.5 grams)
- Milk = 2.5 oz (80 ml)
- Ripe plums (destoned, chopped) = 6
- Non Stick Cooking spray
- Baking paper (for lining the cooker)

For Topping:
- Damson Jam (optional) = 4 – 5 tablespoons (80 – 100 grams)
- Plums (optional) = 2
- Flour = 1 teaspoon (2.7 grams)
- Butter = 1 tablespoon (14 grams)
- Caster sugar = 4 – 5 tablespoons (32 – 40 grams)

Let's Cook:

1. Take out your slow cooker, coat it lightly with the non stick cooking spray.
2. Line the cooker with the baking paper.
3. Firstly mix the butter with the sugar in a bowl. Keep missing until smooth and all the sugar granules are dissolved.
4. Add the eggs one by one and keep beating the mixture in between.
5. Next add the almond extract and baking powder. Mix nicely.
6. Add flour and ground almonds. Mix gently.
7. Stir in half of the chopped plums in this. Now the cake batter is ready. Pour this into the greased and lined cooker pot.
8. Now scatter the remaining chopped plums on the batter. Press them lightly.
9. Close the lid, switch the cooker on and let it cook on high heat setting for 1 – 2 hours or until a toothpick inserted at the center comes out clean.
10. Once the cooking cycle is finished, open the lid and let it cool down a bit. Then take the cake out of the cooker by holding the sides of the baking paper and keep the cake on a rack to allow cooling further.
11. When the cake is cooling down, we can prepare and keep the topping ready. Gather all the topping ingredients. Firstly warm the Damson jam in the microwave. In a small bowl,

combine the butter, flour and caster sugar. Keep rubbing the mixture until it gets breadcrumbs like texture. Chop the plums and place them on the cake. Then drizzle the jam and scatter the sugar mixture as much as needed. Using only the caster sugar as topping also goes well with this cake.
12. Serve it and enjoy.

31. Chocolate Scones

Chocolate Scones are crumbly, moist and bears a supreme taste. Make these chocolate scones for dessert in good quantity, have them to your heart's content, store the left over, have them later and make anytime a dessert time. Having these chocolate scones will lift your mood up and every bite of this scone will make you giggle, feel divine for sure. Make this scone the easy way with your slow cooker and you will be surely inspired to make many more of this and also will inspire others to make this charming dessert.

Preparation Time: 10 Minutes

Cooking Time: 2 Hours

Stand-by Time: 30 Minutes

Recommended Slow Cooker size: 3 Quart

Serves: 8 - 10

Ingredients:

- Self raising = 8 oz (225 grams)
- Salt = a pinch
- Butter = 2 oz (55 grams)
- Caster sugar = 1 oz (25 grams)
- Milk = 5 oz (150 ml)
- Chocolate chunks = 2.6 oz (80 grams)
- Non stick cooking spray

Let's Cook:

1. Take out your slow cooker, coat it lightly with the non stick cooking spray.
2. Now mix the flour and salt together. Stir in butter into it.
3. Next stir in sugar and milk. Whisk well and then knead soft dough.
4. Scatter chocolate chunks onto the dough and again knead it gently.
5. Place the dough into the greased cooker pot carefully.
6. Close the lid, switch the cooker on and let it cook on high heat setting for 2 hours or until a toothpick inserted at the center comes out clean.
7. Once the cooking cycle is finished, open the lid (be careful, don't let any water droplet to drip on the scone) and let it cool down a bit. It should become a little crispy when cool.
8. Slice it into wedges and enjoy the crispy dessert.

32. Crumbled Hazelnut Cheesecake

Hazelnut is believed to be Turkish delight as it is mainly produced in Turkey apart from some other parts of the world. It is good source of oleic acid (the good fat), carbohydrate, protein, vitamins, minerals, dietary fiber, antioxidants and phytosterol etc. So, basically a dessert that has hazelnut is bound to be healthy. Hazelnuts are famous confectionery product that is used to make many tasty bakery items, so the hazelnut cheesecake will be mouthwatering too for sure. The goodness of this dessert will just blow your mind. Have this made by yourself at home with your slow cooker and enjoy.

Preparation Time: 15 Minutes

Cooking Time: 1 ½ - 2 ½ Hours

Stand-by Time: 1 hour

Chilling Time: 3 hours – 3 days

Recommended Slow Cooker size: 5 Quart

Serves: 8

Ingredients:

- Whole graham crackers (crushed) = 6
- Butter (unsalted, melted, cooled) = 2 tablespoons (28 grams) + more for the pan
- Sugar = 2/3 Cup (120 grams) + 1 tablespoon (12.5 grams)
- Cinnamon (ground) = ½ teaspoon (1.2 grams)
- Salt = a pinch
- Cream cheese (softened) = 16 ounces (448 grams)
- Sour Cream = ¼ Cup (60 grams)

- Eggs = 2 large
- Hazelnut Praline Paste = ¼ Cup (62 grams)
- Frangelico Liqueur = 2 tablespoons (30 ml)
- Vanilla extract = 1 teaspoon (5 ml)

For the Crumble:

- Butter (unsalted, softened) = 2 ½ tablespoons (35 grams)
- Confectioner's Sugar = 1/3 Cup (43 grams)
- Hazelnuts (finely chopped, blanched) = 1/3 Cup (40 grams)
- All purpose flour = 1/3 Cup (43 grams)
- Salt (as needed)

Let's Cook:

1. Pour about 2 Cups of water in the slow cooker and place an aluminum foil rack at the bottom of the cooker.
2. Turn the Graham crackers into fine crumbs using a food processor.
3. Take a bowl; Combine the crumbs, butter (2 tablespoons / 28 grams), sugar (1 tablespoon / 12.5 grams), cinnamon and salt (a pinch) in this. Keep whisking until blended well.
4. Rub the extra butter onto a 6 inch springform pan. Transfer the crumb mixture to the buttered springform pan and press gently at the bottom. Wipe out the food processor bowl. Now add cream cheese, sugar (2/3 Cup / 120 grams) and salt (1/4 teaspoon / 1.2 grams) in this and blend them well. Add sour cream, eggs, hazelnut paste, vanilla and liqueur in this. Mix nicely until well incorporated. Make sure not to over mix. Pour this mixture onto the crumb mixture in the pan. Make the top smooth with the back of a spoon.
5. Now place this pan on the prepared rack in the cooker.

6. Close the lid, switch the cooker on and let it cook on high heat setting for 1 ½ – 2 ½ hours or until the thermometer reads 150°F (65°C).
7. Once the cooking cycle is finished, open the lid and let it cool down for 1 hour. You can keep it on wire while cooling down.
8. Wrap the cheesecake with a plastic and keep refrigerator for chilling for minimum 3 hours and maximum 3 days.
9. Prepare the crumble several hours before serving. For this, pre-heat the oven to 350°F (177°C). Rub the butter onto a small baking pan. In a bowl, mix the butter and sugar. Add chopped hazelnuts, flour and salt. Mix well. Spread this on the baking sheet as evenly as possible. Bake this for 15 – 20 minutes or until golden brown and crispy. Take out from the oven and keep it aside. Break them into crumb like pieces when cooled.
10. Now cut the cheesecake, place even layer of crumble on each piece of cheesecake and press gently. Place each piece of cheesecake onto a serving plate and enjoy the satisfying dessert.

33. Pecan Buns

Another dessert with healthy Pecans is here. Pecan buns are sticky, moist, yummy and fully tempting. You will simply love the stickiness of this dessert (just brush your teeth well after finishing it!). It is so easy to make that preparing this dessert with your slow cooker will be your favorite pass time. Just mix up the ingredients, put them in the cooker and go for a nice long shower or get your manicure done or finish any pending work. When the sweet caramelized smell will tempt your taste buds, make a visit to your kitchen to see the dessert is fully ready to be served. Enjoy it with your family members and guests. The recipe is right here for you.

Preparation Time: 50 Minutes

Cooking Time: 2 – 3 Hours

Stand-by Time: 10 Minutes

Recommended Slow Cooker size: 5 Quart

Serves: 12

Ingredients:

For dough:

- Milk (low fat) = 6 tablespoons (90 ml)
- Maple syrup = 4 tablespoons (60 ml)
- Butter (unsalted, melted) = ½ tablespoon (7 grams)
- Vanilla extract = 1 teaspoon (5 ml)
- Salt = ¼ teaspoon (2 grams)
- Yeast = 2 ¼ teaspoon (7 grams)
- Whole wheat flour = 1 ½ - 2 Cups (180 – 240 grams)

For Caramel Sauce:

- Butter (unsalted) = 2 tablespoons (28 grams)
- Milk (low fat) = 2 tablespoons (30 ml)
- Maple syrup = 4 tablespoons (60 ml)
- Pecans (chopped) = ¼ Cup (28 grams)

For filling:

- Maple syrup = 3 tablespoons (45 ml)
- Cinnamon (ground) = 1 ½ teaspoon (4 grams)
- Butter (unsalted, melted) = ½ tablespoon (7 grams)

Let's Cook:

1. Take out your slow cooker, coat it lightly with the non stick cooking spray.
2. We will first make the dough. Gather all the dough ingredients.
   a. Take a microwave safe bowl; Combine milk, butter, maple syrup and vanilla extract in this.
   b. Microwave this mixture for 20 seconds and stir for 1 minute with a spoon. Repeat this until butter melts completely and all the ingredients are combined together nicely.
   c. Add the yeast and let the mixture sit for 10 – 15 minutes. It should become frothy by now.
   d. Add in the flour (1/2 cup / 60 grams at a time) and keep whisking until the dough becomes non –sticky. Place the dough onto a flour sprinkled surface and knead well for

few minutes or until the dough gets s spongy textu[re]. Keep it aside.
3. It's time to prepare the caramel sauce.
    a. Take a pan; Combine butter, milk and maple syrup in this. Heat it over medium-low flame. Stir frequently. Let the butter melt completely. Continue stirring until the mixture thickens and darkens in color slightly.
    b. Pour this mixture into the greased slow cooker. Sprinkle the chopped pecans in the middle portion of this.
4. Let's prepare the filling now.
    a. Take a small bowl; Combine maple syrup and ground cinnamon in this. Whisk nicely.
5. Take the dough and place onto a flour sprinkled surface and roll it into a rectangle of around 10 x 14 inch size. Brush this with melted butter. Pour the filling (cinnamon and maple syrup mixture) on the middle portion of this. Carefully roll it up and seal the edges by pressing on each other. Cut the whole roll into 12 small rolls using dental floss (cutting with knife may cause spilling out of the filling) and immediately place those rolls over the caramel sauce in the slow cooker.
6. Close the lid, keep the cooker heat setting to 'keep warm' mode for 45 minutes or until the small rolls have risen to double of its initial size. Now turn the cooker heat setting to 'low' and let it cook for 1 – 1 ½ hours.
7. Once the cooking cycle is finished, open the lid and let it cool for 10 minutes. Take the pecan buns out. Serve them warm or chilled.

34. Chocolate Cherry Cake

Cake', the name itself is so tempting that it needs ...tion. Once you have this dessert you will know ...chocolate is coupled with sweet cherries how charming it gets. And this super tasty dessert needs just four ingredients and a slow cooker. That's it. Once you get them, you are half way done. Another half of the cooking will be taken care by the slow cooker and you can just chill out and enjoy the dessert. You won't get tired of having this and would crave for more always. So, take a look at its recipe and make it whenever you get a chance.

Preparation Time: 5 Minutes

Cooking Time: 2 Hours

Stand-by Time: 30 Minutes

Recommended Slow Cooker size: 4 Quart

Serves: 4 – 6

Ingredients:

- Chocolate cake mix = 1 box
- Cherry Pie filling = 1 can
- Butter (melted) = 1 stick
- Water = 1/3 Cup (~ 80 ml)
- Non stick cooking spray

Let's Cook:

1. Take out your slow cooker, coat it lightly with the non stick cooking spray.
2. Firstly pour the cherry pie filling in the slow cooker.

3. Sprinkle the whole cake mix powder on this gradually.
4. Melt the butter in microwave or on stove top and add drizzles of this over the cake mix.
5. Cover the crock pot with double layer of paper towels.
6. Close the lid, switch the cooker on and let it cook on low heat setting for 1 ½ hours.
7. Mix the topping package with the water and pour onto the cake in the cooker.
8. Replace the paper towels with new, dry ones. Continue to cook for another half an hour.
9. Once the cooking cycle is finished, turn the cooker off, open the lid and let the cake cool down completely for 30 minutes.
10. Serve this chocolate cherry cake warm with ice cream or with whipped cream or as it is.

35. Cherry Cobbler

Another cherry delight is here. This one is simply delicious yet very comforting. It will make great weekend dessert. This one also needs only four ingredients and has a very short, hassle free slow cooking process. Slow cooker version of cherry cobble is so much adorable that you will cherish its taste for long and would crave for this frequently. Let's peek at the recipe of this zesty dessert and plan to make it on coming weekend.

Preparation Time: 5 Minutes

Cooking Time: 2 Hours

Stand-by Time: Minutes

Recommended Slow Cooker size: 4 Quart

Serves: 6

Ingredients:

- Cobbler Topping (preferably Krustaez) = 1 box
- Cherry pie filling = 1 can of 30 oz (840 grams)
- Butter (unsalted) = 6 tablespoons (84 grams)
- Egg = 1 large
- Non stick cooking spray

Let's Cook:

1. Take out your slow cooker, coat it lightly with the non stick cooking spray.
2. Firstly pour the whole can of cherry pie filling into the greased slow cooker.

3. Take a small bowl; Beat the egg slightly in this. Stir in cobbler topping to the beaten egg and keep whisking until well incorporated.
4. Add drizzle of this cobbler topping mixture over the pie filling in the slow cooker.
5. Melt the butter in microwave or on stove top and spread over the cobbler topping.
6. Cover the crock pot with double layer of paper towels in order to arrest the moisture that builds up inside crock pot while cooking.
7. Close the lid, switch the cooker on and let it cook on low heat setting for 2 ½ hours or until the cobbler is cooked well.
8. If you open the cooker lid in between to check the cobbler, then replace the paper towels with new, dry ones.
9. Cherry cobbler is done. Open the lid of the cooker and let it cool down a bit. Then take it out with spoon.
10. Serve this warm with ice cream. If you wish, you can sprinkle some chopped almonds over this. It adds nice additional aroma and taste.

36. Pavlova with Fruit

Pavlova is a creamy dessert which is believed to have got its name after Russian ballerina Anna Pavlova during her professional trip to Australia and New Zealand. The place of its origin is a matter of argument though. It mainly incorporates meringue (a dessert with egg white, sugar and cream of tartar) like ingredients. It is decorated with fresh fruits and nuts. It looks aristocrat, tastes elegant and feels divine. It's perfect holiday dessert when you are free to indulge in such tasty delicacies. The recipe is simple and the process of making this is even simpler. Just get ready with the chef cap and cook this.

Preparation Time: 5 Minutes

Cooking Time: 1 ½ Hours

Stand-by Time: 30 Minutes

Recommended Slow Cooker size: 3 Quart

Serves: 4

Ingredients:

- Egg whites = 6
- Caster Sugar = 1 ¼ Cups (162.5 grams)
- Corn flour = 2 teaspoons (7 grams)
- Vanilla Extract = 1 teaspoon (5 ml)
- White Vinegar = 1 teaspoon (5 ml)
- Baking paper

For topping:

- Chopped and sliced fruits (kiwi, strawberry, raspberry, blackberry and any other fruits of your choice)
- Whipping cream

Let's Cook:

1. In a bowl, whisk the egg whites nicely.
2. Stir in caster sugar (1 tablespoon / 8 grams at a time) and keep whisking to make sure they mix well and the sugar is dissolved completely.
3. Stir in corn flour, white vinegar and vanilla extract. Keep whisking until well blended and smooth.
4. Line the slow cooker with the baking paper. Pour the batter onto the baking paper carefully so that it does not spill outside the paper.
5. Cover the crock pot with double layer of paper towels in order to arrest the moisture that builds up inside crock pot while cooking.
6. Close the lid, switch the cooker on and let it cook on low heat setting for 1 ½ hours.
7. Once the cooking cycle is finished, open the lid and let it cool down a bit.
8. Top the Pavlova with whipping cream and fruits (slices and pieces) and finally serve.

37. Coconut Cake

If you have guests coming over the weekend and need to make some easy dessert, then consider making this yummy looking, tempting and flavorful dessert. In this coconut cake you can use gluten free cake mix that would make it healthy and using readymade cake mix would spare you from the effort for mixing flour. However, if you are a baking expert and know some tastier alternative, free feel to use that or make the cake batter completely manually at home. So, all set to prepare your first slow cooker version of coconut cake? Believe me; you are going to have fun. Take a look at the recipe before you start cooking.

Preparation Time: 10 Minutes

Cooking Time: 2 – 4 Hours

Stand-by Time: 30 Minutes

Chilling Time: 1 hour

Recommended Slow Cooker size: 4 Quart

Serves: 6

Ingredients:

- Cake Mix (gluten free, for one layer cake) = 1 box (2 boxes for multiple layer cake)
- Oil (as indicated on the cake mix package)
- Butter (as indicated on the cake mix package)
- Eggs (as indicated on the cake mix package)
- Coconut milk = 1 can 16 oz. (500 ml)
- Coconut extract = 1 teaspoon (2 grams)

For Topping:

- Powdered sugar = 2 tablespoons (16 grams)
- Shredded coconut (sweetened)
- Cream cheese frosting (optional)

Let's Cook:

1. Prepare the cake batter as indicated on the cake mix package. Instead of water use coconut milk. Also add the coconut extract to the batter. Reserve the extra coconut milk, if any.
2. Take out your slow cooker, coat it lightly with the non stick cooking spray.
3. Pour the coconut cake batter into the slow cooker.
4. Close the lid, switch the cooker on and let it cook on high heat setting for 2 – 4 hours or until a toothpick inserted at the center comes out clean.
5. While the cooking cycle is on, we can prepare and keep the topping ready. Now mix ½ cup () of the coconut milk that you reserved with the powdered sugar.
6. Once the cooking cycle is finished, open the lid and let it cool down a bit.
7. Poke a few holes in the cake using a skewer and use the sweetened coconut milk and pour it on top. Then Sprinkle the shredded coconut.
8. Let the cake come down to room temperature and then put in the fridge for about 1 hour.
9. Apply frosting if you like and serve coconut cake chilled.

38. Crock pot Apple Pie

Any fruit pie is delicious and rich in fruity flavor. The apple pie is no exception. This dessert is often served with ice cream or cheese and so tastes more heavenly. This dessert can be made in three simple steps and with slow cooker it becomes even easier to cook. Give your evening meal a sweetish touch with this dessert. Take a look at the easy-to-follow recipe and plan to cook this whenever you get a chance. It will be loved by kids as well as elders. Nobody will be able to escape the temptation of the apple pie.

Preparation Time: 20 Minutes

Cooking Time: 6 – 7 Hours

Recommended Slow Cooker size: Quart

Serves: 6

Ingredients:

For the Pie:

- Tart Apples (peeled, sliced) = 8
- Cinnamon (ground) = 1 ¼ teaspoons (3 grams)
- Allspice = ¼ teaspoon (0.5 gram)
- Nutmeg = ¼ teaspoon (0.6 gram)

For Biscuit Mixture:

- Milk = ¾ Cup (187 ml)
- Butter (softened) = 2 tablespoons (28 grams)
- Sugar = ¾ Cup (150 gram)
- Egg = 2
- Vanilla extract = 1 teaspoon (5 ml)

- Bisquick = ½ Cup (60 grams)

For crumb Topping:

- Bisquick = 1 Cup (120 grams)
- Brown Sugar = 1/3 Cup (57 grams)
- Cold butter = 3 tablespoons (42 grams)
- Vanilla Ice cream

Let's Cook:

1. Take out your slow cooker, coat it lightly with the non stick cooking spray.
2. Take a large bowl; Toss the apple slices with cinnamon, allspice and nutmeg in this. All these coated apples to the greased slow cooker.
3. Take another bowl; Combine milk, softened butter, eggs, sugar, vanilla and Bisquick (1/2 Cup / 60 grams) in this. Spoon this mixture over the apples in the slow cooker.
4. Now mix the Bisquick (1 cup / 120 grams) and brown sugar in that bowl. Add the butter. Blend this mixture with a pastry blender until crumbly. Spread this mixture on the apples as well. Sprinkle some cinnamon on top of everything.
5. Close the lid, switch the cooker on and let it cook on low heat setting for 6 – 7 hours or until the apples are soft enough.
6. Spoon the apple pie out from the cooker and transfer to serving bowls and serve with a dollop of vanilla ice cream.

39. Crunchy Chocolaty Nutella Cheesecake

Nutella is branded Hazelnut spread that is sweet and chocolaty. It can be consumed as it is and also can be used to make great desserts. And on the other hand cheesecake seems to be loved by all. It can be made of anything. Now it's time for a Crunchy, chocolaty Nutella Cheesecake that will also be loved by everybody. The combination of tasty hazelnut chocolate spread with Oreo cookies, cream cheese, vanilla extract, whipping cream etc will really make this dessert a memorable one. Making chocolate crust from the Oreo cookies is very creative and this trick lends a special charm to the cheesecake. So, what are you waiting for? Isn't your mouth watering by seeing the description? If so, then get ready to cook this utmost yummy dessert.

Preparation Time: 20 Minutes

Cooking Time: 2 Hours

Stand-by Time: 1 hour

Recommended Slow Cooker size: 5 Quart

Serves: 6

Ingredients:

For Crunch Mixture:

- Crushed Oreo Cookies (need only the chocolate part) = ½ Cup (50 grams)
- Hazelnuts (chopped) = ¼ Cup (30 grams)
- Mini Chocolate chips = ¼ Cup (40 grams)

For Cheesecake batter:

- Cream Cheese (regular or low-fat, softened) = 2 Packages of 8 oz (total 448 grams)
- Nutella (Chocolate Hazelnut spread) = 2/3 Cup (170 grams)
- Egg = 2
- Vanilla = ½ teaspoon (2.5 ml)

For Garnishing (optional)

- Whipped Cream
- Mini Chocolate chips
- Oreo Cookies (crushed)
- Hazelnuts (chopped)
- Chocolate syrup

Let's Cook:

1. Take a small bowl; Combine all the ingredients for the crunch mixture (crushed cookies, chocolate chips and hazelnuts) in this.
2. Now take a large mixing bowl; Combine all the ingredients for the cheesecake batter (eggs, Nutella, cream cheese and vanilla) and mix with an electric mixer at medium speed for couple of minutes or until well mixed.
3. Take 6 glass canning jar. Take spoonful of crunch mixture and place at the bottom of every jar. Distribute half of the cheesecake batter into each jar. Then distribute remaining crunch mixture into jars on top of batter. Then again pour the remaining batter equally on top of second layer of crunch mixture. Make sure the jars are not filled beyond 3/4th of its volume. Otherwise the batter may overflow while baking.

4. Fill the slow cooker with water till ½ inch from the bottom. Place the jar into the slow cooker c carefully.
5. Close the lid, switch the cooker on and let it cook on high heat setting for 1 ½ – 2 hours.
6. Once the cooking cycle is finished, open the lid and let it cool down for about 1 hour. Then Cover the jars and refrigerate overnight.
7. Take out from refrigerator before serving and garnish with all the garnishing ingredients as per your choice.

40. Pumpkin Cheesecake

As I just told, cheesecake seems to be very popular; I found another extremely mouthwatering pumpkin cheesecake recipe for you. In slow cooker, you can cook this pumpkin cheesecake so perfectly that there will be no crack on the top of it, like oven baked cheesecakes do. It will look like restaurant or bakery made cheesecake. It generally is made in a springform pan that is placed inside slow cooker for baking. If you don't possess a springform pan, then you can use a casserole with straight edges. Always grease the pot you are using to make sure that taking out the cheesecake from the pan or casserole does not get messy and does not affect the shape of the cheesecake. Make it for a party at home and be assured it will be a huge hit.

Preparation Time: 20 Minutes

Cooking Time: 4 Hours

Stand-by Time: 10 hours or overnight

Recommended Slow Cooker size: 5 – 6 Quart

Serves: 8

Ingredients:

- Gingersnap cookies = 12
- Butter (melted) = 2 tablespoons (28 grams)
- Brown sugar (packed) = 3 tablespoons (32 grams)
- Cream Cheese (block style) = 2 packages of 8 oz (total 448 grams)
- Sugar = ¾ Cup (150 grams)
- Vanilla = 1 teaspoon (5 ml)
- Pumpkin (canned) = ½ Cup (117 grams)

- Egg = 3
- Cinnamon = 1 teaspoon (2.4 grams)
- Nutmeg = ¼ teaspoon (0.5 gram)
- Allspice = ¼ teaspoon (0.5 gram)
- Sour cream = ½ Cup (120 grams)
- Brown sugar = 2 tablespoons (22 grams)

Let's Cook:

1. Firstly grind the Gingersnap cookies in food processor until they turn into fine crumbs. Mix these crumbs with melted butter and brown sugar.
2. Take a 7 inch springform pan. Grease it with butter or vegetable oil or non stick cooking spray.
3. Press the crumb mixture at the bottom of the springform pan. Let it chill until you are ready to cook.
4. Take a large mixing bowl; Combine cream cheese, vanilla and sugar. Mix them using an electric mixer until smooth enough.
5. Now add eggs, pumpkin, cinnamon, nutmeg and allspice. Keep besting the mixture until well combined, smooth and creamy. Pour this batter into the springform pan.
6. Take two pieces of foil. With one foil cover the pan from bottom through the sides till the top edges. With another foil cover the top of the pan and then press to seal the edges of both foils together. Make sure there is no leakage so there is no chance for water or moisture to leak in or out.
7. Fill the slow cooker with water till 1 inch from the bottom. Place the springform pan inside the cooker carefully.
8. Close the lid, switch the cooker on and let it cook on high heat setting for 4 hours.

9. Once the cooking cycle is finished, open the lid and let it cool down a bit. The texture of the cheesecake improves as it cools down and it gets even better when chilled. So, you may refrigerate it overnight. So, you can prepare one day before when you want to serve it.
10. Before serving take the cheesecake out of the refrigerator. Mix the sour cream and brown sugar. Spread this over the cheesecake. Cut the Pumpkin cheesecake into wedges and serve.

41. Sweet Pecan Candy

Here is another pecan dessert that is crunchy, toothsome and superbly tasty. Whoever eats this dessert just gets addicted to this and never gets tired of munching these sweet pecan candies. Slow cooker made pecan candies are so delightful that you are always crave for them. It will also be perfect dessert item to carry on holidays and also can be served at any holiday gathering. It needs very few, handful of ingredients and can be made very easily using slow cooker. So, make this and enjoy your leisure time.

Preparation Time: 5 Minutes

Cooking Time: 2 ½ Hours

Stand-by Time: 30 Minutes

Recommended Slow Cooker size: 4 Quart

Serves: 12

Ingredients:

- Pecan = 1 bag of 16 oz (448 grams)
- Butter = ½ Cup (112 grams) or 1 stick
- Brown sugar = ¼ Cup (43 grams)
- Sugar (granulated) = ¼ Cup (50 grams)
- Allspice = ½ teaspoon (1 gram)
- Cloves (ground) = ½ teaspoon (1 gram)
- Cinnamon = 1 tablespoon (7 grams)

Let's Cook:

1. Gather and arrange all the ingredients in the slow cooker.
2. Close the lid, switch the cooker on and let it cook on low heat setting for 2 – 2 ½ hours. You can stir occasionally.
3. Once the cooking cycle is finished, open the lid and let it cool down a bit.
4. Then transfer the pecan candies to a sealed jar. Take out before serving and serve as it is.

42. Dulce De Leche

Keeping a jar of sweetened, condensed milk, for using in dessert or having it as dessert regularly, is a great idea. Here is a Latin American sweet dessert dish that is easy to cook and gives you a healthy and comforting treat every time you crave for dessert. The word 'Dulce De Leche' means 'candy made of milk'. It has a creamy soft yet crumbly texture. It is a popular dessert in various parts of the world. It has many versions also depending on the place and available ingredients. In Mexico, goat milk is used whereas in Cube they soured milk (curdled) which is then sweetened. Like this it has got many makeovers and every time it tasted equally divine. We will see a basic recipe of 'Dulce De Leche' here. Let's go through it.

Preparation Time: 5 Minutes

Cooking Time: 8 - 10 Hours

Stand-by Time: 30 Minutes

Recommended Slow Cooker size: 4- 6 Quart

Serves: Depends of the use

Ingredients:

- Milk (sweetened, condensed) = = 2 cans each of 14 ounce (420 ml)
- Canning jar = 3 each of 8 ounce

Let's Cook:

1. Firstly open the can of sweetened, condensed milk and pour the milk in the 3, 8 ounce jars. Distribute equally. Close the lids of the jars and put on the rings.
2. Place the jars inside the crock pot and keep pouring water slowly until the water level reaches the bottom bands of the jars.
3. Close the lid, switch the cooker on and let it cook on low heat setting for 6 – 8 hours if caramel sauce like consistency is needed. Otherwise Continue to cook till 10 hours if pudding like consistency is desired. It should get nice brown color by now. While slowly cooking the condensed milk, a reaction called 'Maillard Reaction' takes place that changes the color, flavor and texture of the condensed milk.
4. Once the cooking cycle is finished, open the lid and let it cool down a bit.
5. Then carefully remove the jars from the slow cooker. Serve this as it is or serve with fruit slices.

Printed in Great Britain
by Amazon